CHILDREN
OF THE SUN

his honor and as a memorial of his faithfulness, the Indian uses
the turkey wing to make his fire burn.

THE SIMPLE HAPPINESS
OF A NAVAJO GIRL

My mother's hogan is dry
against the gray mists
of morning.

My mother's hogan is warm
against the gray cold
of morning.

I sit in the middle
of its rounded walls,
walls that my father built
of juniper and good earth.

Walls that my father blessed
with song and corn pollen.

Here in the middle
of my mother's hogan
I sit
because I am happy.

(Excerpt from Ann Clark, *Little Herder in Spring*, Bureau of Indian Affairs,
Chilocco, Oklahoma, 1940)

CHILDREN

OF THE

SUN

Stories by and About

Indian Kids

ADOLF and BEVERLY
HUNGRY WOLF

WILLIAM MORROW AND COMPANY, INC.

New York

Library of Congress Cataloging-in-Publication Data

Children of the sun.

1. Indians of North America. 2. Indians of North America. I. Hungry Wolf, Adolf. II. Hungry Wolf, Beverly. III. Title.
E98.C5C44   1986   970.004'97   86-18285
ISBN 0-688-06782-4

Printed in the United States of America

First Edition

1 2 3 4 5 6 7 8 9 10

BOOK DESIGN BY BERNIE SCHLEIFER

Contents

Introduction 9

ONE: **A CHILD IS BORN** 15

Winnebago Birthing, Naming, and Adoption 18
Red Leggings, and More Adoption 19

TWO: **GROWING UP OUTDOORS** 24

Young Hunter of Picuris 29
Training of a Flathead Girl 30
Omaha Care and Training of Children 32
Ancestral Embers 36

THREE: **INITIATIONS TO TRIBAL MYSTERIES** 38

How Children Receive Blessings 40
A Winnebago Boy's Initiation 43
Poor Wolf Joins a Hidatsa Boy's Society 44
Daughters of Ponca Chiefs 46
A Girl Joins a Mandan Women's Society 47
Fasting Customs Among Winnebago Children 48
Omaha Ceremony to Honor a Young Girl 49

6 *Contents*

Children of the Iruska   51
A Sioux Boy as Heyoka   52
Clowns Among the Crow Tribe   53
Hosteen Klah: Boy Medicine Man of the
    Navaho   56

FOUR: STAYING ALIVE   59

My Indian Grandmother   60
An Omaha Boy Gets Native Doctoring   61
A Hidatsa Childhood in the 1860s   64
Childhood Quotes   67
Goodbird Is Nearly Drowned   69
The Pawnee Girl Who Saved a Prisoner   87
Riding a Dog Travois   90
Games Played by Omaha Children   91
A Taos Schoolboy at Home for the Summer   96

FIVE: FINDING A MATE   99

Omaha Marriage Customs   102
Winnebago Marriage Customs   104
Sioux Maiden's Feast   105
Hidatsa Courting Customs   108
Courting at the Corn Harvest   109
Courting in Sioux Tipi Camps   110
Blackfoot Tipi-Creeping on the Canadian
    Prairies   114

SIX: SOME CHILDHOOD STORIES   116

A Typical Summer Day for a Hidatsa Boy   116
Childhood Memories of Willie Eagle Plume   125
The Debut of Aloyasius   133
The Return   138
Little-Joe's Back Home   142
The Conversion of a Dozen Young Hopis   144

Little Taos Boy at a Dance   146
A 1950s Child of the Sun   148
A Sun Dance Child of the Blackfeet   175

SEVEN: TALES FOR THE FIRESIDE   180

Manitoshaw, the Hunting Girl   182
The Poor Turkey Girl   188
Coyote and the Fawn's Stars   195
Coyote and Crow   196
Blackfoot Legend of Napi and the Great Spirit   197
Napi and the Elk Skull   198
Napi Makes Buffalo Laugh   199
Origin of Names Among the Cherokees   199
Why the Turkey Is Bald   202
The Simple Happiness of a Navaho Girl   203

Introduction

We are all Children of the Sun; the title of this book is meant as a tribute to *all* of us. From the Sun comes light and warmth to make life grow. All our human ancestors walked in awe of the Sun, although modern life often lets us—their descendants—forget about that.

North America's original Children of the Sun were Indian tribes who roamed the plains, mountains, forests, and desert sands, building simple homes and living in harmony with nature. Some of them did this so recently that being in awe of the Sun is still part of the heritage handed down among today's generations of Indian people. We offer the following information and stories in support of that heritage, one which we also try to teach our own children.

By presenting colorful narratives from earlier generations it is not our intent to make you long for the past. We are approaching the twenty-first century; the world has been irrevocably changed from the childhood times recorded in this book. But the changes seem to have little value in helping our offspring feel like Children of the Sun, and we think that's too bad. So many children grow up feeling lost and alienated in today's world. These stories might help some of them—and their parents—better appreciate where we are all coming from.

We especially offer these stories for younger members of Indian tribes to encourage them to feel good about their native heritage, also to remind them how closely they are descended from our land's original Children of the Sun. We know that young Indian people face the same daily challenges and distractions from modern life as their non-Indian neighbors and cousins. Public schools, television, popular music, complex toys, even the English language, have together captivated most Indian children so that there is little space left in their minds for thoughts about ancestral heritages and simple traditions.

However, we think that people of *all* backgrounds can enjoy and learn from these stories. Everywhere there is a shortage of successful families to serve as role models for the young of today. Many of us parents want to make the lives of our children more meaningful than were our own, yet we have few examples to go by. Let these stories, then, be such examples.

The most important theme is that of families working closely together to survive the constant challenges of life. We still have constant challenges—though they may appear different at first glance from those of the tribal past—but we often face them as individuals, rather than as families united in the same cause.

Think of *your* family life as you read along. Are there things you could be doing with your family that might bring about a more united feeling? Camping is great for that; so is the planting, growing, and harvesting of food. How about building a home together, or part of one? All the families you're going to read about did these things together. They joined one another in frequent and sincere prayers, in wonderful sessions of singing and telling stories, and in journeys of adventure and discovery around their nearby lands. Families of today can still do all these things together, if they want to!

We began to study the material in this book some years ago

as part of our own efforts at living as a unified family, following a simple life-style and practicing some Indian traditions. So far we've been successful at raising four of our children in a wilderness cabin, without TV or telephone, but with plenty of camping, planting, and singing of songs. Perhaps the time will come when we can write out a full report of our experience, but for now we are all still in the midst of doing it, and learning from it. We are still far from being "experts" at child raising, or even in the telling of personal childhood lore. That is why we offer the following accounts, from those who have gone ahead of us.

As part of our evening entertainment we have read these accounts aloud at home, commenting on them afterward. Those we've selected to include in this book were the ones that were received with the most enthusiasm. As an Indian child growing up in the 1950s, Beverly had her own comments and stories to enliven our studies. She has also spoken with many elders (mostly from the Blood tribe of Alberta) in an effort to learn some of the things children felt and experienced in the generations between her own and those of the earlier tribal days.

We urge parents everywhere: Look closely at your family life and see where you can give it more time and energy. If you agree that there are greater challenges coming in the years ahead than we have ever seen, you will surely want to help prepare your family to face them, together. May our presentation give you ideas, inspiration, and encouragement.

The authors wish to thank the Canada Council for support in preparing part of this project.

CHILDREN
OF THE SUN

CHAPTER ONE

A Child Is Born

A child is born. It is cleaned. The umbilical cord is coiled in a circle—a symbol of the circle of life—and tied. The midwife is careful not to cut this cord too short when she separates the child from its mother. Then she diapers the child, using an extra-soft piece of hand-tanned hide lined with a soft, absorbent plant, such as moss or sage, or else a layer of powdered buffalo dung. Then she wraps the child with a piece of old, soft hide, tying it with a leather cord. Finally she gives it to the mother, who holds it to her breast for its first real taste of life.

That is the way our family's grandmothers described the birth of a Blackfoot child "back in the old days." Other Indian tribes had their own customs for childbirth, but there was a basic similarity to them all. They were simple, without much special comfort or glamour. There were no adjustable beds, drug injections, disposable diapers, or feeding formulas. It was childbirth at its most natural and sensuous, but also at its deadliest. In fact, infant mortality rates were so high in the "old days" that the stereotype of "big" Indian families crowded into tipis and lodges was certainly not due to husbands and wives having and raising many children! The average Indian woman appears to have thought herself lucky to raise three or four kids to adulthood!

Once the child was born, mother and child experienced a unique sort of togetherness for a month, since tribal custom decrees that they should stay in seclusion until the passing of a moon, dressed in old clothes and avoiding social gatherings and public notice. This was a trying period for the health of the mother and child back when life was often harsh and always rugged. It seems almost as though the tribe did not want to recognize the birthing until time showed it to have been successful.

At the end of its first moon the child was given a "coming-out party." This could be quite an event, *if* things were going well for the family at that time, for they had to provide a feast and presents for guests. Relatives and elders were invited to the family lodge after it was first thoroughly cleaned by the family's women, then purified with incense.

Mother and child were dressed in new clothes for this special occasion. Everyone was given an opportunity to lavish praise and prayers upon the infant. Often the event was also used to announce its name, usually one given during that day by an especially notable person in the crowd. Gifts were given to the visitors, with the name giver receiving the best and greatest number of them. In that way the people came to know the new little persons within their midst, receiving a bit of happiness and reward at the same time.

The close interrelationship between young and old, as exemplified by the naming feast, is the key to success in the traditional life of our Children of the Sun. It is *this* key that is virtually unknown in so much of modern society, where kids often have little chance to know their own parents, much less a supporting cast of related elders. Count yourself very fortunate if your family life includes both children and elders.

Old Indians of the past fifty years often said young women have babies much more often now than they did back in the old days. There has been an unprecedented population growth among Indian tribes.

"Survival of the fittest" is no longer the basic theme of Indian life, at least not in the original sense. As parents (and as former children!), we can only be glad for that. But now we must instead grapple with modern society's problems. Surviving no longer means getting enough food and shelter, at least not for most Indian families; rather it means a constant battle with myriads of distractions and problems unheard of back in the time of our great-grandparents.

A WYANDOT CRADLE SONG

Hush thee and sleep, little one,
     The feathers on thy board sway to and fro;
The shadows reach far downward in the water,
     The great old owl is waking, day will go.

Sleep thee and dream, little one,
     The gentle branches swing you high and low;
The father far away among the hunters
     Has loosed his bow, is thinking of us now.

Rest thee and fear not, little one,
     Flitting fireflies come to light you on your way
To the fairy-land of dreams, while in the grasses
     The merry cricket chirps his happy lay.

Mother watches always o'er her little one,
     The great owl cannot harm you, slumber on
Till the pale light comes shooting from the eastward,
     And the twitter of the birds says night has gone.

(Excerpt by Hen-toh from "The Red Man," Carlisle Indian School student newspaper, Carlisle, Pennsylvania, c. 1925)

WINNEBAGO BIRTHING, NAMING, AND ADOPTION

When the time for delivery came, it was the custom for the woman to occupy a small lodge erected especially for her use. None of her male relatives were permitted to be present and her husband was not even permitted to stay at home. He was supposed to travel continually until the child was born, in the belief that by his movements he would help his wife in her delivery. According to one informant the husband had to hunt game, the supposition being that this procedure on his part would cause his wife to have enough milk for the child. This traveling of the husband was called, therefore, "Looking for milk." It was considered improper for a woman to cry out during labor pains, and by doing so she subjected herself to the jests of her elder female relatives. The cradle-board was always made before the child was born.

The positions commonly assumed by women in delivery may be described thus: Supported by the arms, which were passed over a pole held in the crotches of two forked sticks driven into the ground; suspended between two stakes; or flat on the back.

The infant's navel string was cut off and sewed into a small bag, which was attached to the head of the cradle-board.

On the birth of a child the sisters of the husband were supposed to show his wife especial marks of courtesy. They always gave her valuable gifts, such as goods or a pony. They were glad that he had offspring, the people said, and even permitted their brother's wife to give the presents received from them to her own relatives. The presentation of these gifts was called "Cradling-the-infant." Gifts were presented also to the wife's brothers.

(Excerpt from Paul Radin, *The Winnebago Tribe,* Thirty-seventh Annual Report of the Bureau of American Ethnology, Smithsonian Institution, Washington, D.C., 1923)

THE NAMING FEAST

The clan name was generally bestowed on a child at a special feast held for the purpose. . . . The bestowal of the clan name was not infrequently delayed by a father's inability to gather the requisite amount of food to be presented to the old man who was to select the name. Occasionally it even happened that a father under such conditions permitted the relatives of his wife to bestow a name on a child, which of course was a name from its mother's clan. . . . A person possessing no clan name was regarded as having low social standing.

ADOPTION

Adoption of individuals was quite frequent among the Winnebago in former times. As far as the writer knows, however, it always took the form of replacing of a deceased child by some other child physically resembling the one lost.

. . . A special feast could be given for adoption or it could be done at one of the regular feasts. As the child adopted was often the "friend" of the deceased and in any case had parents living, presents were always given to his parents.

In the words of an informant: "When a child dies, then the father mourns for many years, and if during that time he happens to meet a child that resembles his dead child he asks to be allowed to adopt him. The parents of the child can hardly object to such a request."

RED LEGGINGS, AND MORE ADOPTION

The elders we've known all told us, "It's good to have lots of kids, so there will be someone around to look after you when you are old." Even in today's modernized Indian society you seldom find old people left alone. In how many non-

Indian towns would you find the still-common reservation
scene of a young couple driving a flashy new car while an old
grandma sits in the backseat wearing head scarf and a shawl?
Grandparents will even go to rock dances with their grandkids.
We know one who did so in his eighties, and he got out on the
floor to dance!

Red Leggings and his wife were an old, childless couple on
the Blood Reserve around 1920, at the time when Beverly's
mother, Ruth Little Bear, was a little girl. They were old folks
from the buffalo days, living in a log cabin not far away. When
they got lonesome, old Red Leggings would hitch up his team
and wagon and go pick up Beverly's mother, whom they knew
only by her Indian name, Pretty Crow Woman. She said, "He
used to tell me, 'Come on with me, your grandma has baked
you a pie,' though he said it in Indian. What she had made was
ordinary oven-top bread with some raisins sprinkled in. I
would stay with them for a while, maybe overnight; they
treated me like a little princess. They were just like a form of
grandparents, although we weren't actually related."

Among the Bloods the name of a famous head chief of the
buffalo days is still with us because he adopted a little mixed-
blood orphan boy who grew to old age and left a large family,
which carries the chief's name as their own last name. Other
children sometimes teased this boy because of his light skin
and European features; they often called him "white man
child." Whenever the boy went and told his father, there was
always trouble for the teasers, since the man was head chief.
He truly loved this light-skinned orphan boy.

This boy, incidentally, had a twin brother, who was
adopted by a noted family among our northern Blackfoot divi-
sion, the Siksika. Interestingly, both boys grew up to become
tribal chiefs themselves, within their separate divisions.

There are many recorded instances of non-Indian children
being adopted by Indian families. A famous example is the
mother of Quannah Parker, himself a renowned chief of the
Comanche at the end of the buffalo days. Cynthia Parker was a

young girl when her parents were killed during an Indian raid. She was spared and brought to the Comanche camp, not as a slave, but to be raised with the other children of her captor, as part of his family. She later married a tribal leader, with whom she had Quannah Parker.

Although Indian tribal life emphasized love and need for children, there were also instances of child neglect, abuse, and even murder. In some of these cases tribal customs were involved, while others were the result of emergencies, such as enemy attacks or widespread starvation, as occurred now and then in the buffalo days.

For instance, a distant relative of our family's was a fearless warrior who sometimes brought his wife along on his enemy raids. We don't want to give his name because his descendants might not like this story, but it illustrates what kind of extremes Children of the Sun were once faced with—and perhaps still are today, among some hard-pressed people.

This relative was out on an open trail, traveling with his wife and a few others, searching for buffalo on the prairie. Before they knew it, they had wandered into the midst of a large and scattered enemy encampment. They were still unseen, so their only hope was to conceal themselves quickly in dense brush lining a nearby streambed and wait there until darkness would let them escape. For this, they knew they would have to remain completely silent and unseen.

Unfortunately, our relative's wife was quite pregnant at this time, and the excitement brought on labor. She gave birth right there, in hiding, to a lively and squalling child. Since people from the enemy camp were continually coming down near the hiding place for water, the group knew it was only a matter of time before someone would hear the baby's cries, and then they would all be discovered. Even if not then, the baby would likely attract attention from camp guards later on, when the group planned its escape. In addition, everyone needed to be ready for action at all times, which was not possible around a newborn baby. With much sorrow from the parents, the group together agreed that the newborn had to be smothered. Such circumstances were not unusual back in the wilderness days.

Children who were born with defects usually did not live long. If the mother saw that the deformity was hopeless, she often took the infant out to the bushes or forest and left it to die. Someone else might do this for her instead. Generally nothing was said against this in any tribes. The rugged life-style often left no choice in the matter.

Some particularly proud fathers wanted nothing but sons, and were known to order their wives to take girl infants outside and abandon them. There is yet a very old woman alive in the Blackfoot tribe who was said to have been treated this way. Such action was tolerated, though not without criticism. Often the abandoned babies were taken up and adopted by relatives, or other adults, as was the case with the old lady of our acquaintance. Of course, there are also many legends about such babies being rescued and raised by wild animals, which might really have been possible back when everyone was completely wild.

It was not unusual for mothers, as well, to get sick or die from the effects of giving birth. The rugged life-style and lack of modern medical techniques left little room for difficulties. It was again a "survival of the fittest." If the infant stayed alive without its mother, it was usually given to another family with a new baby, at least long enough each day to nurse, though often permanently.

A grandfather of Beverly's lost his mother at birth, back in the late 1800s, when she couldn't expel the afterbirth. Herbal medicine and massage were both tried, in an effort to save her, but nothing helped. One of his grandmothers immediately adopted the infant and brought him around to other young mothers so that he could nurse from them. She also let him nurse on her own wrinkled breasts, which finally gave forth a bit of milk from the stimulation. She was said to be immensely proud of this, so that it became a well-known story.

This grandfather was also fed broth by his grandmother, as

were other children in cases of milk shortage. When we first got married and lived in a log house on the Blood Reserve, our neighbor and landlord was an old widower who had been similarly fed as an orphan. In our time he carried the last name of Soup, on account of this.

In this century there has been a population explosion among Indian tribes that has brought about drastic changes in life-styles. Many factors have contributed to the increase, including better health and welfare and the elimination of many physical dangers. The strong influence of the Catholic church among many tribes prevented the acceptance of birth control when it became available. Only in recent years has public education affected this trend, with the result that there are now new Indian generations who want to have only one or two children instead of a houseful.

Parenthood is planned these days, which is very different from the old way of having families, but there are still important events among many tribes for celebrating the birth of a new member. It is to be hoped that parents of today, who are able to choose when to have children and how many to have, will devote enough time and energy to making sure those children are well guided as they grow up. To start with, parents could plan on engaging in many outdoor family activities, thus assuring our primeval inheritance as Children of the Sun.

CHAPTER TWO

Growing Up Outdoors

Childhood in tribal camps and villages flowed in very natural rhythms, without much of the structuring that often gives today's children stress. Indian children's relationships with family, friends, and spiritual matters were usually taught with very strict discipline, but most of their day was spent freely, learning to flow with their big, outdoor world of nature.

Traditional camp life provided children with role models —heroes and heroines—who helped set and maintain high standards in many tribes. Brave warriors and hunters, wise chiefs, and sacred women were all held in high public esteem, so that most of the tribe's children strove to emulate them.

Of course, back then the requirements for success in life were quite basic and simple: Get food, have warm clothing and shelter, protect the tribe from enemies and bad weather. It didn't take a school degree to learn that, although tests were frequently given and failures often punished by death!

Those are still our basic needs in life, today, but modern children are often so distracted by all our material accumulations that they hardly recognize basic needs. Among some tribes there are predictions of a major event coming soon to the world to remind everyone of basic needs, again. How would today's youth fare in the event of a catastrophe?

Camp life was easily learned by every child, since it went on continually all around him. Children learned first by watching, then by imitating at play, and before too long by actual participation. Boys at ten or twelve were hunting, even fighting enemies, while girls of that age helped cook and tan hides, preparing soon to be married.

An infant's first introduction to discipline came in the form of cradleboards and moss bags. An Indian baby spent very little time unbundled, lying out open, or left to crawl around in a big space. Scientists can probably make all sorts of deductions from the different practices, but we must at least recognize that children laced securely into bags start out life learning how to be still!

The cradleboard was a secure place for a baby to live during its transition from the mother's womb to walking about in the open world. For a people without cars and bassinettes, it was also a very compact and handy baby crib. We used moss bags and a cradleboard for all our children and found this to be a really safe and secure way to handle infants, even in modern times.

Our cradleboard was a very pretty one, beaded with colorful floral designs by a cousin. It was handy for going on walks, when Beverly carried it on her back with a wide leather strap, or for traveling by truck. It fit nicely between our seat and the dashboard and seemed fairly protective.

But for everyday use we found moss bags far more practical. Each of our kids had their own, decorated with different beaded designs. Along with the cradleboard, these are now heirlooms—as they often were in the past—to be used by whatever child comes next into our family.

A moss bag resembles a soft shoe, made big enough for a baby to fit in and laced up the front with strings of buckskin. In the past these bags were made of hand-tanned deer and antelope skin, but in recent years some of the nicest ones we've seen were made of velvet.

Ironically, one traditional thing we didn't put into our moss bags was the substance from which they got their name. Moss was used in place of diapers, and it seems to have worked at least as well. We learned about it from Beverly's aunt, Mary One Spot, who also made our first moss bag.

Aunt Mary said that for her own kids she and Uncle Frank would go out into the forest to pick the moss from pine trees, where it grows. They would get a big sackful of it at a time. At home they would clean it carefully by hand, picking out all the pine needles and sharp sticks. A big bunch of it was then packed around the baby before it was laced into its bag. This could soak up a lot of moisture before it needed changing, at which time the really soiled parts simply peeled away from the baby's skin, leaving it practically clean.

Aunt Mary's people are the Sarcee, who live by the mountains where there are pine trees. Their Blackfoot neighbors and relatives spent more time out on the prairies, so they used sage leaves, also powdered buffalo dung, for their diapers. Another source was powdered punkwood, which was also used in place of talcum powder.

A child's next discipline, after the moss bag and cradleboard, usually had to do with toilet training. This was started when a child was able to sit, then encouraged even more when it began to crawl. Children able to walk were in all cases expected to make their toilet away from the home. Some parents told their kids something like, "If you leave it close around here, the boogeyman will come after it and get you, too!" The enforcement of these practices varied from family to family and tribe to tribe, just as it does among all other people.

The act of first-walking was, itself, a cause for special celebration among some tribes. In one, this celebration was held when the child made its first lone journey on foot to a neighbor's home, that neighbor then being obligated to provide everyone with a feast.

Walking children were, of course, more troublesome than bundled-up infants, which is why some mothers kept their children in cradleboards pretty long. Supervision of toddlers was often provided by other children around the household, but certain rules had to be taught to small children very quickly if they were to survive. For instance, it usually required one, and only one, burn for a child to learn that it must stay back from fire. Other things were learned more slowly.

Physical punishment was not common in most Indian households. Because there were usually several grown-ups on hand, a disobedient child could expect quick disapproval, either in words or by sounds, such as "tss-ss," which seemed to get attention about as quickly as a slap. In some tribes it was all right to slap a child, in others a willow stick was considered proper for the purpose, while among our own family's elders all forms of physical punishment were frowned upon for children.

A naughty Blackfoot child might hear a common threat like, "Hey, Coyote, come and eat this bad boy." Little kids were quite familiar with the howlings of elusive Mr. Coyote, and in their minds it seemed within reason that such a critter could be called in to bite them. Some tribes had a particular boogeyman, or another, whose name was called for help in settling a misbehaving child. Sometimes a neighbor dressed up and acted out the part, thereafter making the idea seem even more real.

One of our elders experienced a form of tribal discipline for children that no one practices today. Every morning, as a young boy, Willie Scraping White was forced to join a couple of others in a run to the nearest water, where they jumped in for a refreshing dip. This was especially vigorous when the wind was blowing, at twenty or thirty below, and a hole had been chopped through the ice to let them at the water!

Willie Scraping White lived to be ninety-seven, and he said this early practice toughened his body and helped him to grow so old. He said it also taught him to obey orders, since the morning ventures were supervised by an old man who walked with a long stick and was known for taking no nonsense. Besides teaching the boys to be brave and tough, this old man also taught them what might happen if they were to misbehave at some other time of the day. Scraping White considered himself and his friends always well behaved!

Religious discipline was of vital importance for the children of most tribes, since there were usually strict taboos against the mistreatment of religious ceremonies and articles. For instance, most Blackfoot households had one or more medicine bundles hanging at the back, in the place of honor. Children were taught from the start not to go near these, or to throw anything at them.

When we were being shown how to look after our family's medicine bundle, it was stressed that children must act respectful around it, which is harder to do in this age of undiscipline. Paula Weaselhead, herself a former bundle keeper, said that she kept her kids from disturbing the family's sacred area by spreading in front of it the hide of a wild animal of which her children were afraid.

Yet, in the traditional home, children usually became involved in the family's spiritual practices right from the start, so that it was not long necessary to worry about their mistreatment. Instead, children acquired further self-discipline as they gladly sat and kept quiet for long periods at a time, in return for hearing stories and songs or for being allowed to watch their elders performing colorful ceremonies.

Religious teachings, like other training in Indian life, were passed on through the generations by means of active participation, beginning with earliest childhood. This is true of traditional life-styles all over the world, including such more modern ones as farming and ranching, at least until recent times.

YOUNG HUNTER OF PICURIS

They went outside.
In the clean snow,
    Grandfather made
    some turkey tracks.
Young Hunter was excited.
    "I've seen those.
I know what they are," he shouted
    and off he started running,
    holding out in front of him
    his bow and arrow.

Grandfather called after him,
    "Are you picking berries
    with the women
    that you need to make such noise?
Perhaps you shout
    to warn the game away
    from such a dangerous hunter."

Young Hunter came back.
He stopped running and shouting.
He watched his grandfather.
He watched him taking quiet steps.
Then he, too, took quiet steps
    and together they went
    hunting for turkey.

(An example of traditional Indian "teaching" is given in the following excerpt from Ann Clark, *Young Hunter of Picuris,* Bureau of Indian Affairs booklet, Haskell Institute, Lawrence, Kansas, 1943)

TRAINING OF A
FLATHEAD GIRL

Our family used to have an adopted grandmother among the people of the Flathead tribe, who live south of us, in Montana. Mary Ann Combs was born in a tipi along Montana's Bitterroot River, in 1881. For the first ten years of her life she was among those few Flatheads, with her parents and other relatives, who shunned reservation life in favor of their ancestral wilderness homeland. In her old age, eighty or ninety years later, she was the last one of her tribe who had received the traditional training that brought her from childhood to becoming a woman.

Mary Ann grew up in the lodge of her grandparents, who wanted to make sure she would learn to be a woman in the true, proven, old Flathead way. Thus, when she reached puberty, they asked a highly respected old woman to be her guide. This woman, Mrs. Ninepipe, was noted for being a hard worker and a good wife and mother, as well as being kind and helpful to others in the tribe.

Mrs. Ninepipe went to visit Mary Ann early on the first morning of her instructions. She began with a lengthy prayer, asking that the girl have a long life as a good woman. Everyone who knew Mary Ann felt that this prayer came true. The woman gave Mary Ann additional blessings by painting her face with a red-colored earth that her people considered sacred.

Then she said, "You have to watch me and see how I live. I don't flirt or run around with men. I work hard to gather roots and berries, and to prepare all the meat that my husband brings home. I save everything I can and don't waste things. I know that my husband provides the family with food and protects us, so I follow his orders like a dog does its master, and I do what he wants me to do."

For the next four days Mary Ann stayed with Mrs. Ninepipe and did exactly as she was told to do. She was required to work hard during that time and she was not allowed to rest. Her father and mother warned that she should obey everything the old woman told her if she wanted to have the old woman's virtues in later life.

The people near her were part of a hunting camp of four lodges. She was required to bring a load of firewood to each of the lodges every day. She carried these loads on her back, in the old way. She was also told to bring the water supply for each lodge. In addition, she was required to do all the cooking in the lodge of her parents, without help from anyone else.

She said, "That old woman told me the reason she wants me to keep busy and working is so that I don't start out being a lazy woman, else I would have scabs all over my body—even on my face—and I would become lousy and filthy and would always want to lie around. I was pretty scared about being this way, so I kept busy all the time I was with that woman.

"She taught me to prepare bitterroots the right way, and she told me never to be careless about it. She said to watch so that I don't waste food, or let it get overcooked. She showed me how to make our traditional blood soup without breaking up the blood too much. She said that if I was careless making this nutritious soup, the blood would turn into water.

"She told me not to warm my feet by the fire, else they would grow large as I got older. She said to warm a rock and hold it to my feet instead. You can see that I have small feet. She also told me that if I had any lice, I should take one and stick a pine needle through it and then stick the pine needle into the ground by the fire to roast the louse. She said that way I would never be bothered by lice, and she was right.

"Every morning I was told to get up very early and wash myself in the creek and put lots of water on my hair so that it would grow long and heavy [Mary Ann's thick, white braids still hung below her waist when she was in her eighties]. I was told not to wash with warm water or in a basin. That is why I still go down to the little creek behind my house every morning to wash."

Mary Ann was also given instructions for having children. She should never eat the flesh of the black bear or her breasts would go dry. Also, she was not to pick berries from bushes in which grizzly bears had fed, else the child she was carrying would always have saliva running from its mouth, like a bear.

She was told different ways of giving newborn babies certain characteristics, according to Flathead belief. To make a baby grow up quiet and gentle, she was to take the heart of a partridge, mix it with a certain white clay, and frequently rub the mixture on the child's chest. To make a child active, industrious, and grow up to be a good food hunter, she was told to crush a bunch of ants and mix them with white clay, to be rubbed on the child's chest. To make children brave, they should be rubbed with mixtures containing the hearts of hawks or eagles. To make them strong, the mixture should include part of a bear's heart. To make them good hikers and climbers, she should use the heart of an elk. Her husband, Louie Combs, had been rubbed with a mixture that included a chipmunk's heart, which made him always slim and frisky.

Mary Ann said that she continued helping old Mrs. Ninepipe for the rest of her life, in thanks for the guidance given her while she was young. In her own old age she believed that if the young people of today were still given such strict and direct training at the hands of elderly wise persons, they would grow up to have more respect for life and better behavior.

OMAHA CARE AND TRAINING OF CHILDREN

In the Omaha family the children bore an important part; they were greatly desired and loved.... The baby was its

(Excerpt from Alice C. Fletcher and Francis La Flesche, *The Omaha Tribe,* vol. 2, Twenty-seventh Annual Report of the Bureau of Ethnology, Smithsonian Institution, Washington, D.C., 1911)

mother's constant companion, although other members of the family often helped to take care of it. More than one instance is recalled where the father took considerable care of the little ones and it was not an uncommon sight to see a father or grandfather soothe or amuse a fretful child.

Soon after birth the baby was laid in its own little bed. This was a board about 12 or 14 inches wide and 3 feet long. On this was laid a pillow stuffed with feathers, or the hair of the deer, over which were spread layers of soft skins. On this bed the baby was fastened by broad bands of soft skin, which in recent years were replaced by similar bands of calico or flannel. There was no headboard to the Omaha cradleboard, but the skins that were laid over the pillow were so arranged as to form a shelter and protection for the top of the baby's head. While the child slept, its arms were bound under the cover, but as soon as it awoke they were released.

The cradleboard was principally used in carrying the baby around and it served as a bed when the little one was asleep. A good portion of the time the baby lay on a soft skin in a safe warm place where it could kick and crow, while the mother sat by with her sewing or at some other employment. If the mother's duties took her out of doors the baby might be laced on its cradle and hung up in the shade of a tree; or if the mother happened to be going away on horseback the baby in its cradle was hung at her saddle, where it rode safely and comfortably.

When the child was old enough to cling to its mother it was thrown over her shoulder, where it hugged her tightly around the neck while she adjusted her robe or blanket. The robe worn by the woman was tied by a girdle around the waist, the upper part was placed over the clinging child, and the ends were crossed in front and tucked into the girdle. Then the mother gave a gentle but decided shrug, when the child loosened its arms and settled itself into its bag-like bed, from out of which it winked and peered at the world, or fell fast asleep as the mother trudged about her business.

It is a mistake to suppose that Indian babies never cry. They do cry, most lustily at times, but efforts are always made to soothe a child. Both men and women make a low murmuring that resembles somewhat the sound of the wind in the pines, and sleep soon comes to the listener. There was a belief that certain persons were gifted with an understanding of the various sounds made by a baby; so when a little one cried persistently, as if in distress, some one of these knowing people was sent for to ascertain what troubled the child. Sometimes it was said that the baby did not like the name given it and then the name would be changed.

The birth of twins was considered a sign that the mother was a kind woman. It was said, "Twins walk hand in hand around the world, looking for a kind woman; when they find her, she becomes their mother."

As soon as a child could walk steadily it passed through the ceremony called Turning the Child, and, if a boy, through the supplemental ceremony of cutting the lock of hair in consecration of its life to the Thunder, and to the protection of the tribe as a warrior. After this experience home training began in earnest.

Careful parents, particularly those who belonged to the better class, took great pains in the training of their children. They were taught to treat their elders with respect, to be particular in the use of the proper terms of relationship, to be peaceable with one another, and to obey their parents. Whipping was uncommon and yet there were almost no quarreling and little downright disobedience. Much attention was given to inculculating a grammatical use of the language and the proper pronunciation of the words. There was no "baby talk." Politeness was early instilled. No child would think of interrupting an elder who was speaking, of pestering anyone with questions, of taking anything belonging to an older person without permission, or of staring at anyone, particularly a stranger. Yet the children were bright and had their share of curiosity, but they were trained not to be aggressive.

Little girls were subject to restraints that were not put upon the boys. The mother was particular in teaching the girl how to sit and how to rise from a sitting posture. A woman sat sidewise on the left, her legs drawn around closely to the right. No other posture was good form for a woman. Sometimes old women sat with the feet stretched out in front, but that was the privilege of age. All other attitudes, as kneeling and squatting, were only for temporary purposes. Concerning this point of etiquette, mothers were rigid in the training of their daughters. To rise well, one should spring up lightly, not with the help of both hands; one hand might be placed on the ground for the first movement.

A girl was taught to move about noiselessly as she passed in and out of the lodge. All her errands must be done silently. She must keep her hair neatly braided and her garments in order. At an early age little girls assumed the role of caretaker of the younger children.

The boys had to help about the ponies but not much training in etiquette fell to the lot of the boy—he could jump about and sit in any manner he chose, except after the fashion of a girl. Later he had to learn to sit steadily on his heels, to rise quickly, and to be firm on his feet.

When quite small the two sexes played together, but the restraints and duties put on girls soon separated them from the boys, and when girls were grown there were few recreations shared in common by the sexes. In olden times no girl was considered marriageable until she knew how to dress skins, fashion and sew garments, embroider, and cook. Nor was a young man a desirable husband until he had proved his skill as a hunter and shown himself alert and courageous.

Politeness was observed in the family as well as in the presence of strangers. The etiquette in reference to the fire was always observed (children didn't walk in front of adults), and care was taken not to interrupt a speaker, and never to accept anything from another without recognition by the use of an expression the equivalent of "thank you."

ANCESTRAL EMBERS

Parents and children seem to get along well as families when they camp and hike together outdoors. Communication between old and young becomes much easier, away from traffic and TV, sitting together under the shade of big trees, on top of some hill or mountain, by the site of a lulling stream. We hope the stories in this book will inspire those of you with children to go outdoors more often with them. Let your hearts open to each other as they open to the spirits of nature.

We see embers from our ancestral past residing within the hearts of everyone. *You* have felt them glowing more strongly when you've gone outside to nature. Can you remember those special feelings you got with your first look at some hidden lake, down into a wild, rugged canyon, or up at a spectacular waterfall? How do you feel when you hear wild geese making their peculiar cries as they fly northward across the skies? Children are born to respond to natural environments. We adults need to encourage them to recognize these ancestral embers, while at the same time trying to make them glow more strongly within ourselves. What better source of energy could we have for strengthening relationships between kids and their moms and dads?

Family life for children back in tribal days meant having many "brothers and sisters," even if these weren't necessarily all siblings. Cousins were called brothers and sisters, as were the children of cousins, and also the cousin's wife's cousins. In addition, nonrelated lifelong friends called each other brothers and sisters, as did the children of such friends. Perhaps we might put this example to use in these days? Are you willing to discipline yourself to think of close friends and relatives as brothers and sisters, and to treat them accordingly? Are you willing to explain this to your children and encourage them to do the same? Imagine if we could make this a popular custom!!

Beverly recalls her young days in a tribal society as an extended-family life-style. Strong bonds of mutual assistance and affection were the general rule. It was not uncommon for eight or ten people to live closely crowded together in the family's log house, as it had been among earlier families living in tipis. Many nights she shared her narrow bed with two or three other kids, or with adults. She didn't know the luxury of a private bedroom, or even a private space. From these experiences she learned to share, and to accept her share.

Little brothers and sisters lived together like a litter of pups, sleeping and nursing together, in warm weather often running naked to save wear and tear on clothes. But when they got to be about six or seven, their free relationship ended. From there on it was pretty much intertribal policy to have boys and girls keep separate except to get married.

One obvious reason for separating boys and girls was to lessen the chances of incest. Another was to keep boys from developing too much interest in the more peaceful pursuits of girls. Homosexual boys were accepted among most tribes—in a few they were even held in mystical esteem—yet parents preferred their sons to grow up as traditional men, able to hunt and fight, and to mate with women in order to have children.

The training of younger children was often carried out by the older ones. Children learned to respect those who were older than they, even if only by a few seasons. This kind of respect is still very evident in many Indian tribes today. We think it would benefit young and old alike if other youths could learn this example from tribal life.

CHAPTER THREE

Initiations to Tribal Mysteries

Above all else, childhood in America's native tribes meant being raised with spirituality. The daily life of tribal children was as filled with religion as that of Amish youths in Pennsylvania or Catholic ones in Rome. Religious rules generally dictated each tribe's do's and don'ts, so these were learned by children right from the start.

However, there is a major difference between the organized religious life of Europeans and the generalized spirituality among America's natives. That difference is perhaps best illustrated by the complete absence in native languages of the word *religion*. Traditionally speaking, tribal religion was the same as tribal life; the two were not consciously separated.

Instead of written books to give explanations for the universe and its mysteries, native peoples on this continent relied on ritual initiations and endless oral sessions to pass their own tribe's explanations and understandings from one generation to the next. This process began right after birth and lasted through to death. It was part of life for every single native child, just as surely as eating, sleeping, or growing old. In fact, there were prayers for each of these activities, and for nearly

everything else in life. There was a continuous acknowledg-
ment of greater Powers, and this gave children an unquestion-
ing, lifelong faith that is virtually impossible to find nowadays
in our confusing world.

A native child's first initiation often came within weeks of
its birth and involved its receipt of a name. This event is com-
parable to church baptisms. Native children of modern times
often receive both kinds of blessings, their parents finding no
conflict between the new and the old.

Children often show their need for wanting "to belong."
Initiations and society memberships answered this need within
many tribes, some of whom have continued these traditions
without interruption, while others have lately tried to revive
some of them from the past. It is unfortunate that modern
schooling and entertainment have distracted so many children
from their traditional ways, even when such were offered to
them, although some tribes have been much less affected in
this than others.

Our own children have gone through quite a number of
traditional initiations with various members of our family and
tribal elders. So far, we are pleased with the faith they continue
to show, even while modern attractions also appeal to them.

Among the following stories we hear first from Porcupine
Woman, the widow of a kindly medicine man named Bob
Black Plume. As spiritual leaders within the Blood tribe of Alberta, they were among those who gave initiations to our own
children, along with many others.

In her talk, Porcupine Woman tells with pride (in her native Blackfoot language) how her children "grew up in the Indian way," which included initiations to ceremonies she herself
went through as a child. Now in her eighties, she was the "favorite child" (*minipoka,* in Blackfoot) of her father, a leading
medicine man, doctor, and ceremonialist named Flint (or, on
official records, Tough Bread).

HOW CHILDREN RECEIVE BLESSINGS

I was my father's *minipoka*—his indulged child—as was the custom in our tribe. He picked me because I was the first of his children to survive; the others before me had all died. The older people of that time were so concerned about me that they were going to cut off one of my fingers as an offering, over which they were going to mourn. This was often done in the past when a family had hard luck with children. They said mourning at birth meant they would not have to mourn again, later. This was done for Wolf Old Man, who died just a few years ago at the age of nearly one hundred.

But my father loved me too much to allow this kind of suffering. Instead, the old women in the crowd took me and pierced my ears. This was done for good luck, using sharp rose thorns.

My father treated his grandchildren the same way he had treated me. My firstborn was a daughter, and my parents would barely let me take care of her. They would call me whenever she needed nursing, but otherwise they kept her close by them. Of course, in those days we all lived closely together, even though we had log houses instead of tipis. My parents lived next door to us at that time.

Some old women pierced my daughter's ears before she even saw the light of her first morning, although my father again tried to stop this because he didn't want to hear the baby cry. My mother right away made a pretty moss bag in which my little girl was kept tightly laced most of the time, making her easy to take care of. This bag was made of red wool decorated with colorful beadwork. Inside, the baby was wrapped in soft cloth. For diapers, my mother used the traditional material—dung from the prairie, crushed and powdered so fine that

(Told on the Blood Reserve in 1985 by Porcupine Woman, or Mrs. Bob Black Plume)

it never bothered the skin, and it never seemed very soaked.

We have a Blackfoot word for a "favorite child," and it means in English "beaded person." That is because the favorite children always dressed really fancy; they were given beaded moccasins, dresses, belts, leggings, vests, and things like this, while other kids wore plain leather things, or store-bought clothing of material.

My mother hired Dick Soup's wife to help make my first child a beaded outfit when she got old enough to go to dances and ceremonies. Dick Soup was my husband's brother—their dad had two wives, and those were their mothers. This lady was known for fine beadwork, and soon my little girl had a fully beaded belt, purse, and moccasins that were matching. The moccasins even had the soles fully beaded, to show how special she was! The background was blue, and there were colored Indian designs, and she sure looked good. When she got dressed up like this for the first time, they brought her to Big Eagle, and he transferred a topknot to her. This was a strip of wild-animal fur tied to her hair in a certain way to show that she was initiated to the Medicine Pipe ceremony. From there on she was allowed to attend these ceremonies whenever they were held, and this was done to add value to her life and prayers.

Later, when I had my first son, he was also taken over by my mother. She made him a new moss bag, a very special one. The front of it was of tanned otter hide, and the back was of weasel skins sewn together in strips. The rounded part on the bottom, where his feet rested, was also made of weasels, white with the little black tip.

My mother used to dress all my children in a similar fashion. One daughter had a beautiful cloth dress covered with elk teeth, the other had a dentalium-shell cape. My father was the leader of many ceremonies, and he liked having his grandchildren dress up in our old Indian style to attend. He would paint their faces with sacred earth, and each time this was a blessing for their lives. He was sharing his prayers and ceremonies with them, and that is how they started to learn our original life.

Nowadays I see a lot of young people in the tribe who have only English names. I made sure my children were given Indian names from the start. These are the names we use in our prayers. These are the names my children grew up with at the beginning, and this gave their lives more meaning. For instance, my oldest daughter's name is Nutamotpoiski, which means something like Making-nice-sounds-in-the-morning. The old lady Kills-for-Nothing named her from the Sun Dance. As she was laying holy one time during that sacred ceremony—fasting—she heard this very special sound, and so she gave it to my daughter through the name.

You should know that Kills-for-Nothing was a very holy woman, even with her name. This name was given to her for good luck when she was just a baby, long before she became a Sun Dance woman. The one who gave the name was a brave man in battles, so he passed on the good luck with the name. The old lady named my daughter even before she was born. She used to say, "Why is Making-Nice-Sounds-in-the-Morning not being born? I am anxious to go find a son-in-law!" Of course, she was just joking.

When my baby was a bit older, my father went to old Kills-for-Nothing and told her, "All right, now I'm asking you to properly name this child." So the old lady came to our home and performed the ritual. She used yellow earth paint on my girl's face—she put on a design from her own dream, and that was good luck. She prayed hard and long, while the rest of us watched. To show appreciation, my father tied a nice spotted horse in front of the door for the old lady, and on its back he put a new Hudson's Bay blanket.

All my children were "tied." We say they were tied, because sacred necklaces were put around their necks to give them blessings. Some of these were Sun Dance necklaces, made by the holy women who put up the Sun Dances. They used hairlocks, blue beads, and white shells. These are symbols from the Sun Dance. With each necklace was good luck from the Sun Dance. The holy women were sharing their blessings by tying my children.

Sometimes, when my mother fixed new moss bags for her grandchildren, she went to the leaders of ceremonies and got braids of sweet grass or bunches of sweet-pine needles, which they used for making incense and prayers. She sewed these into the moss-bag linings, and this was another way of sharing blessings with children. These are some of the ways of our first people; the white ways are only very recent, and the children now grow up very differently from my time and the times before me.

A WINNEBAGO BOY'S
INITIATION

I was about thirteen years and over when they told me that they would make me a member of the medicine dance. I liked it very much. Some people do not like it at all when they are asked to join the medicine dance (because of the strict initiations). Very much did my parents desire me to do it. If I wished to live a holy life, that is what I should do, they told me.

This ceremony molded me. I paid the most careful attention to it; I worshiped it in the best way I knew how. I was careful about everything in my life. I never drank liquor. A holy life it was that I sought and most earnestly did I pray that I might live over again. That is what I yearned for. If I do everything that this ceremony enjoins upon me well, I will return to Earthmaker, they told me. This is what I wished. I was doing well as a medicine man and everyone loved me. This ceremony was made with love.

If at any time any of my leaders in the medicine dance

(Excerpt from Paul Radin, *The Winnebago Tribe,* Thirty-seventh Annual Report of the Bureau of American Ethnology, Smithsonian Institution, Washington, D.C., 1923)

wished to give the ceremony I would stay in his house together with those who had been invited. I would do all the work for him, sing the medicine dance songs, etc. All the different things he was supposed to do, all that I would do for him.

When his wife cooked, I carried the water for her, I made the fire, and helped her with the dishes. All the work she liked to have done in the house, I did for her.

All the clothes I possessed I gave to him. Money I gave to him, and the food he needed I procured for him. Whenever he gave a feast, in addition to what he cooked, I would put a special pail of food on the fire for him. When he ate it he was thankful.

One day he said to me, "My son, you have been treating me very well. Even my own brothers never treated me the way you have been doing. I thank you. All my relations hate you, but don't pay any attention to them. You are from a different family and I am teaching you various things, they say. They want me to stop instructing you. My father left the medicine dance for me to take care of. I am in complete control of it. . . . My ancestors would say that you are my relative for what you have done. . . . My knowledge of this ceremony belongs to you, for you have paid for it. My remote ancestors told their descendants, as it has passed down from mouth to mouth to us, that whosoever pays careful attention to all that pertains to this ceremony, that whosoever has a good memory, he is the one to whom it should be taught. Thus they spoke."

POOR WOLF JOINS A
HIDATSA BOY'S SOCIETY

When Poor Wolf was seven years old, he joined the Notched Stick society. Together with other boys of about

(Excerpt from Robert H. Lowie, *Societies of the Hidatsa and Mandan Indians,* American Museum of Natural History, New York, 1913)

the same age, he bought the privileges of membership from the group of older boys then in possession of them. For twenty nights the buyers were obliged to entertain the sellers. On the twentieth night a woman was made to stand up by the sellers; she held in her hand a bundle of willow twigs, painted red at the top and enclosing a central stick of greater length, which was spotted in the middle. This woman danced, and the buyers were obliged to pile up property until the heap reached the woman's forehead. The sellers tried to press down the heap of goods, while the buyers tried to swell it as high as possible. When the pile had reached the required height, the goods were removed, and the process recommenced until four piles had been accumulated and taken away. The buyers sometimes added a tent (or tipi) in order to increase the height of a pile. Poor Wolf's group was assisted in this purchase by members of some higher group, who considered themselves friends of the buyers. . . .

During the twenty nights preceding the consummation of the purchase, the sellers discussed matters with the buyers, and instructed them about warfare and other affairs. The final step was taken when each boy, on the last night, approached an individual of the upper grade, this selecting him for his "father," and presented him, according to his means, with a horse, a gun, or a bonnet. Each novice was free to select whomsoever he pleased for his special father, though the entire group stood in the relationship of sons to the entire group of sellers. The son approached his father and said, "My father, you must give me a feather to tie to my head." The father, if sufficiently distinguished, might fulfill the request himself, otherwise he would call upon a brother of his, who thus addressed the son: "After belonging to the Notched Stick society I did so-and-so (describing a brave deed in battle)." He then tied a feather to the novice's head, told him of a vision received by himself, gave him his own paint, and expressed the hope that the boy would grow up to be an old man and would be successful on the warpath.

At the time of the smallpox (in the mid 1800's), most members of the Notched Stick society died, including Carries-arrows, in whose earthlodge the meetings were held. Poor Wolf's group never sold the membership to a younger generation, hence Poor Wolf, aged 90, still considers himself a member of this society.

DAUGHTERS OF PONCA CHIEFS

A man who was working up to the chieftainship and who had joined many different societies and had been a brave, next had his daughter tattooed. He prepared a large feast, got together 100 awls, 100 knives, 100 black silk scarves, 20 or 30 blankets, 2 strands of sleigh bells, 100 plates, killed two buffalo and got their grease, prepared two large pipes and two extra ones and provided tobacco and kinnikinick, set up a large tipi, and ordered two women to cook the feast. They, of course, had to be dressed well and feasted at his expense. He next asked all the chiefs to fast and tattoo his daughter. The wives of the chiefs and other guests sat in a circle outside the lodge, and were also feasted. Each tattooer received a horse with saddle and bridle.

Sometimes several men joined and all had their daughters tattooed at once. Tattooed women (a small blue mark the size of a dime was made on the forehead, between the eyes) formed a sort of a society, and were privileged alone to wear soft-soled moccasins of a certain . . . type. They were the socially elect of the tribe.

There was great rejoicing, drumming, singing, and dancing at these feasts. After it was over a herald announced that the giver was half a chief.

The next step towards the chieftaincy after having one's

(Excerpt from Alanson Skinner, *Ponca Societies and Dances,* American Museum of Natural History, New York, 1915) daughter tattooed, was to have her ears pierced. The chiefs were again called in, and those who did the piercing each received a horse. A feast was given and many blankets distributed.

A GIRL JOINS A
MANDAN WOMEN'S SOCIETY

The White Buffalo Cow society was the highest of the women's societies known to the Mandan and Hidatsa.... The leader was an elderly woman wrapped in the skin of a white buffalo cow. Only the older members had the tattoo marks between mouth and chin that were distinctive of the society....

Calf-woman joined the White Buffalo women when she was only two years old. Two years later she began to take part in the performances. Some old women went round the village looking for a female child whose parents loved her dearly and had given away a great deal of property in her honor. They came to Calf-woman's parents, and these consented to have their daughter adopted. Calf-woman's mother gave Brave-woman one pony and several blankets on this occasion. Whenever there was a dance of the society, a member named Berry carried the newly adopted infant on her back. There were about fifty women members, and five men acted as singers. The most important dance, or ceremony, of the society took place once a year, in the winter, on four successive nights. Sometimes the dance was kept up every other night for a month.... The object of the ceremony was to lure the buffalo....

Any old member (of the White Buffalo Cow society) could adopt as many new ones as she wished, and was obliged to provide each with a headdress (made from a strip of skunk

---

(Excerpt from Robert H. Lowie, *Societies of the Hidatsa and Mandan Indians,* American Museum of Natural History, New York, 1913)

skin, with feathers attached). Calf-woman obtained one of
these headdresses at the time of her adoption, though she was
only two years of age. She became a middle officer because her
adoptive mother (the old member) gave her the appropriate
calfskin robe.

FASTING CUSTOMS AMONG
WINNEBAGO CHILDREN

From the age of five, children, male and female, were
taught the customs of their ancestors in a series of talks always
delivered by an elderly male relative, perhaps the father. The
specific training differed, of course, for boys and girls and for
individuals. Personal training ceased at the age of puberty,
when all, both boys and girls, were sent out to fast. For boys
this fasting constituted the only puberty rite. After their faces
had been blackened with charcoal they were sent to some
neighboring hill with the injunction not to return till dawn.
Gradually they would be sent out for two, then three, nights; if
after that trial they were not blessed they would be advised
either to desist entirely or exhorted to fast until they were
blessed, no matter how long the time required to secure the
desired result. While fasting the boys and girls used the following formula (or prayer): "Spirits, am I likely to be blessed?
That is why I am praying."

One old Indian informed the author that in former times
the young boys and girls were offered either bread or charcoal
for their fast. If they took the charcoal, well and good; but if
they took the bread, they were unceremoniously kicked out of
the house and the charcoal was thrown after them. From other
statements of this informant one might gather that the young
. . . generally took the bread. . . .

(Excerpt from Paul Radin, *The Winnebago Tribe*, Thirty-seventh Annual Report of the Bureau of American Ethnology, Smithsonian Institution, Washington, D.C., 1923)

A faster is always told to be careful as to what kind of spirits bless him, as he might be blessed by a bad spirit. Therefore a faster's blessings are always reviewed by the elders. Old people used to call the children in at dusk, as the evil spirits were said to be around then.

. . . My informant was of the opinion that the parents purposely treated their children roughly, so that they might feel all the more miserable while fasting and thus pray all the more intensely.

All boys do not seem to have approached the ordeal of fasting with the proper religious feeling. One instance in particular showed anything but a reverent attitude; this is so amusing that it is here given in the exact words of the Indian: "When I was a young boy, my folks made me fast together with a boy named Modudjeka. We were supposed to go to the hills and cry until the spirits blessed us. However, whenever we looked at each other and at our charcoal-blackened faces we could not refrain from bursting out laughing. Whenever we made up our minds to cry, something would induce us to look at each other and the laughing would begin all over again. When the time came for our return to the house, we didn't present the slightest indication of having cried, so we took some saliva and made long streaks on our faces."

OMAHA CEREMONY TO HONOR A YOUNG GIRL

Omaha families of high standing went through a complex series of ceremonies, including one that brought lifelong honor to a selected girl. Usually this was the eldest daughter of the family, but if they had none, the daughter of a relative or even

(Information from Alice C. Fletcher and Francis La Flesche, vol. 2, *The Omaha Tribe,* Twenty-seventh Annual Report of the Bureau of Ethnology, Smithsonian Institution, Washington, D.C., 1911)

a close friend was so honored instead. In either case, she had to be a virgin, one who had recently reached puberty. For her, the high point of the ceremony was a ritual tattooing, by which she was tribally considered to have received the "mark of honor."

The girl was specially dressed for this event in an elaborate outfit made of new, clean leather. Over her dress she wore a soft-tanned robe that was embroidered in colorful, symbolic designs with porcupine quills.

Upon entering the ceremonial lodge, which was crowded with notable members of the tribe, the chosen girl was required to perform a sacred dance, which "dramatized the awakening of the feminine element—an awakening everywhere necessary for a fulfillment in tangible form of the life-giving power."

Usually one of the tribe's chiefs performed the tattooing. Among the fees paid by the girl's family for this honor were to be one hundred knives and one hundred awls, considered to be male and female implements, thus adding to the event's symbolism. The work itself was done with the aid of steel needles tied together in a bunch. Small bells were fastened to this bunch to intensify the pain. In earlier days flint points were used instead of needles, and the rattles of rattlesnakes took the place of bells.

The designs were first traced on the girl's skin with a flattened stick dipped into a solution made from crushed charcoal. After the design was pricked into the skin with the needles, more charcoal was applied. A round spot on the forehead represented the Sun and was always done first. A special song was sung for this. Next, a large, four-pointed star was placed on the girl's chest, again to the tune of a special song.

Other designs used on these occasions included crescents for the Moon, which were placed on the back of a girl's neck, along with turtles, which were put on the backs of the hands. During these proceedings the chosen girl was expected to make no sound or outcry of pain. If the tattoos healed quickly, this was considered a good omen for her life.

CHILDREN OF THE IRUSKA

In this organization there were but six or seven members. They carried quivers full of arrows which were very highly prized, so when an arrow was shot they went to hunt it. They were known as "saaro," youths.

They did things by contraries. If a woman said, "Do not get water," they went after it. They were given to playing the wheel game and because of their peculiarities no one played with them. If an enemy attacked the village, the members would continue to play the wheel game and pay no attention to the fighting. If a person came up and said, "Do not go out to fight," they rushed out at once. They were always painted black as if ready to fight. On the head each wore the skin of a blackbird. The society is said to have been handed down by this bird. The leader so appointed by the bird went through the camp and selected boys who seemed queer, or even insane. These he organized into a society.

They did not go into a fight until they were told not to; then they simply shot their arrows toward the enemy without taking much aim and then went to get them; or in other words, an idiotic performance. At all times of their lives they did things in reverse order. They never married or had anything to do with women. Whenever strange or mysterious animals were reported which were feared by other people, they would try to kill them. It is said that the society became extinct by all being killed in a battle except one, who afterwards disappeared.

(Excerpt from James R. Murie, *Pawnee Indian Societies,* American Museum of Natural History, New York, 1914)

A SIOUX BOY AS HEYOKA

One time when I was about 13 years old, in the spring of the year, the sun was low and it threatened rain and thunder, while my people were in a camp of four tipis. I had a dream that my father and our family were sitting together in a tipi when lightning struck into their midst. All were stunned. I was the first to become conscious. A neighbor was shouting out around the camp. I was doubled up when first becoming conscious. It was time to take out the horses, so I took them.

As I was coming to my full senses I began to realize what had occurred and that I should go through the heyoka ceremony when fully recovered. I heard a herald shouting this about, but am not sure it was real. I knew I was destined to go through the heyoka. I cried some to myself. I told my father I had seen the thunder: "Well, son," he said, "you must go through with it." I was told that I must be a heyoka, if so I would entirely recover. If I did not go through the ceremony, I would be killed by lightning. After this I realized that I must formally tell in the ceremony exactly what I experienced.

I also saw in the dream a man with hair reaching his heels while all over his back were many birds moving about. He was painted red; on the arms and legs were longitudinal marks with forks at the ends. On his face were live tadpoles and dragon flies. He carried a sinew-backed bow with four red arrows. In one hand he carried something covered with horse flies; it seemed afterward to be a dew-claw rattle.

In the heyoka I was ordered to array myself as nearly like this dream man as possible. So I had a long-tailed bonnet made and covered the tail with feathers. On my face and body I painted tadpoles and dragon flies. In one hand I carried a dew-claw rattle and a string of the same over the shoulder.

When everything was in readiness, I came out and danced

(Told by Calico, age sixty-eight, of the Oglala Sioux, excerpted from Clark Wissler *Oglala Societies,* American Museum of Natural History, New York, 1916)

around through the camp with other heyoka, sounding my rattles and dodging about. While this was going on a cloud came
up and threatened rain, but after we stopped it broke away.
Then I took off my regalia in the ceremonial tipi and some old
heyoka took the things out to a high hill and left them as an
offering. They said I did very well. . . .

After this I did not feel uneasy and afraid because of a
threatening storm. Hence I believed there was much truth in
the teachings.

This is the way one must do. He must make a feast and in-
vite the heyoka. Thus I did. I told them all about my dreams.
Then two heyoka took me in hand, arranged my regalia, gave
me instructions and saw me through.

Now, there are two kinds of heyoka, one kind are crazy and
foolish. I was of this kind. When they take in new members,
they fill a kettle with boiling meat. Then all thrust in their
hands to grab for the finest pieces. They have two kettle bear-
ers to bring the kettle into the ceremonial tipi. The heyoka
dance around it, singing heyoka songs. They select roots to
chew and rub on their hands and bodies; this is medicine. As
the leader sings all get ready and baring their arms crowd up
around the kettle, joking with each other. One will dip up
water out of the kettle in the hollow of his hand and dash it in
the faces of the others. Then they plunge their arms into the
kettle and grope around in the soup. I went through with this.
The medicine keeps the water from scalding.

CLOWNS AMONG THE CROW TRIBE

The man who takes the initiative in the arrangement of the
performance (of clowns) bids his friends meet in the brush,
bringing with them gunnysack, mud, and leaves. They make

(Excerpt from Robert H. Lowie, *Societies of the Crow*, American Museum of
Natural History, New York, 1913)

leggings of gunnysack and one-piece shirts with an opening for the head. Mud is used instead of body-paint. A mask is made out of cloth, slits being cut for the eyes and mouth, and is blackened with charcoal. . . . The nose is sometimes fashioned out of mud and stuck on, at other times it is simply marked with charcoal. When the clowns have disguised themselves so as to be quite irrecognizable they leave their hiding-place and approach the camp.

As soon as the people catch sight of them, they cry, "The (impersonators) are coming!" The clowns walk as if they were lame and act as clumsily as possible, so that the spectators cannot refrain from laughing at them. The people crowd in on the performers to watch their antics. One of the clowns is dressed up as a woman, wearing a fine elk-tooth dress; he is obliged to walk, talk, and sit like a woman, and is stuffed so as to simulate pregnancy. Among the clowns there is a singer who has been provided with a torn drum, the worst that could be found. . . .

The clowns attempt to make fun of any one they like, regardless of his distinction, because everyone is laughing at them. The spectators try to identify the actors and to inform one another who they are. Then the clowns act like monkeys. They talk to one another in whispers and bid one another dance so as to make the people laugh. In addressing the crowd they disguise their voices. As soon as they see the singer pick up his drum, they walk about, preparing to think up some antics. The singer takes up his drum as if to beat it, but merely rattles it, at the same time heaving a grunt. The impatient onlookers cry out, "Dance, we wish to see you dance!"

The clowns have prepared willow bows and arrows, or worthless old firearms, with which to frighten the people while dancing. When starting out on their expedition, they have selected and abducted the ugliest horse, crooked-legged and swollen-kneed, that they could find. Ugly as it is, they have tried hard to enhance its unattractiveness by turning down its ears and tying them with willows, plastering its face with mud or masking it, and putting gunnysack leggings on its legs. Slits are made in the mask for the eyes. The owner of the horse does not know it has been stolen until he sees it in the public performance, where it appears ridden by the "woman," who sits behind another clown. This rider with his arrow or gun motions to the spectators, signaling to them not to press too close but to keep their distance. Usually the people heed these admonitions, which are seconded by the "woman." When the drum is finally beaten, the clowns scatter, each dancing as ludicrously as possible. After a while the drummer gets excited and throws his drum away on one side and his drumstrick in the opposite direction. He then begins to dance all alone without any music.

When his companions see him acting in this fashion they likewise recommence to dance without drum or chant. Finally all the performers stop except one clown who refuses to cease dancing and thus attracts the attention of the spectators, who cry out, "There's one dancing still!" The other clowns turn around. Then the horseman bids his companion dismount and dance, but "she" refuses and clings to her partner, who becomes enraged and pushes her head, whereupon she gets down and begins to dance. Her companion now makes preparations to dismount, but purposely falls off and pretends to be badly hurt. After a while he dances with his weapons, then he proceeds to get on horseback again, but intentionally overleaps so as to fall, and again acts as if seriously injured.

Some wags in the audience are in the habit of asking questions and making such remarks as, "These fellows must have come from a great distance." The clowns answer by means of signs that they have come from very far indeed and are tired out as a result of their journey; sometimes they say they have come from the sky. Then someone may ask, "How many nights did it take you to get here?" By way of reply the clown begins to count up to hundreds and hundreds, and would never stop were it not for the drummer, who seizes him by the back, saying, "You are mad, you do not know where we have slept." Then he throws him down. The clown pretends to fall headlong, but stops after a while, and begins to laugh. In fact he pretends to die laughing and kicks his feet up in the air. . . .

Little boys, as well as older ones, crowd about, trying to identify the performers and pelting them with dung. While the outsiders are being held off by the horseman, the clowns make a run for the thickest part of the brush in order to prevent recognition, doff their costumes, dress in their usual clothes, scatter in all directions, and at last slink back into camp.

In July 1911 a group of young boys dressed up as clowns one afternoon and rode to the dance house, where a performance of the Hot Dance (a popular native dance) was going on. They dismounted, entered, and, to the amusement of the spectators, began to dance.

HOSTEEN KLAH:
BOY MEDICINE MAN
OF THE NAVAHO

Hosteen Klah was one of the most highly recognized Navaho Indians during his era, which spanned from the late 1860s to 1936. He was considered the most knowledgeable medicine man among his people, having mastered several very complex ceremonials, each one lasting some days and nights. That he learned the first of these before he was even ten years old makes him something of a genius in the culture of his people.

Many boys the age of Hosteen Klah were taken away to U.S. government schools, where they were taught to forget their own culture. But Klah's family had too much pride in the traditional ways to let him wander away from them. Instead, he became sort of a crutch and right-hand man for an aged uncle who lived in the household, and who happened to be the most noted leader of the Hail Chant, one of the complicated ceremonials, this one for curing certain sicknesses.

(Information from Franc Johnson Newcomb, *Hosteen Klah,* University of Oklahoma Press, Norman, Oklahoma, 1964)

The uncle took his young nephew along whenever a family hired him to perform the Hail Chant. He and Klah traveled widely over the desert to reach the various places. Along the way they sought various medicine plants, which the uncle showed the boy how to dig up, store, and prepare for aiding the sick and injured.

After a few years young Klah was sent south from the land of his people to the Apache, ancient relatives, to one of whom his aunt was married. Her husband was a leader of the Wind Chant, which was similar among both people. The complex ceremony lasted five days and nights, during which the leader had to sing many sacred songs and perform numerous ritual details, all in proper order.

This Wind Chant had to be performed for Hosteen Klah by his Apache uncle, after a bad riding accident left the boy with numerous injuries, among them a broken collarbone. During his period of healing, Klah managed to learn the details of this ceremony from his uncle.

While Klah was a helpless invalid from his accident, it was discovered that he was a hermaphrodite. Among his Navaho people, this made him a distinguished person, someone held in awe. He was considered to have been especially honored by the spirits for receiving attributes of both men and women. He was thenceforth expected to master both men's and women's skills, and he did so with perfection. Besides learning the complex ways of being a medicine man, he also gained wide fame as the weaver of very high-quality wool rugs. Many are now prized in the collections of museums.

By the time Hosteen Klah returned from the Apache to his own Navaho people, he was a teenager, and already he had some fame among them for ceremonial knowledge. At home, the uncle who had taught him the Hail Chant was too feeble to lead the ceremonial anymore. All he could do was accompany the boy and give him background guidance. By coincidence, the first ceremonial that Klah performed in this way was for a nine-year-old boy, only a few years younger than he.

The Hail Chant was being performed for this boy because

he had been struck by lightning while herding the family's sheep. He had managed to get the sheep under a big cedar tree, where they were somewhat protected from the rain and hail. He had then crawled underneath a big ewe in the herd, hoping she would provide him with shelter. But when lightning struck the tree, it knocked him unconscious. He was found by his father, who carried him home. When he finally regained consciousness, the boy could no longer talk.

During the days and nights of this ceremony, Klah had to make seven intricate sand paintings illustrating the various spirits involved in lightning and rain. Each detail had to be done from memory, and absolutely correct. After the ritual, each painting was destroyed. Parts from medicine bundles were used in combination with herbs, songs, and prayers. On the final day of the ceremony the stricken boy stepped through the smoke of herbal incense, then turned to Klah and others of the gathered crowd and said, "I am all right now. *Yata-hey!*"

When word of the success reached others in the tribe, the future of Hosteen Klah as a medicine man became assured. There are yet today young Navaho boys who receive ceremonial training from older relatives, like Hosteen Klah from his uncle. To them, he remains the greatest symbol of the ability to find success within their own tribal culture.

CHAPTER FOUR

Staying Alive

We originally planned to call this chapter "Health and Welfare," until we realized that the whole thing boiled down to a "Survival of the Fittest." Thus we simply say, "Staying Alive."

This is the topic that frightens away the romantics among you, who read the other sections and say, "Gee, it would be nice if we could go back to the old Indian days." The going was more tough then, to put it mildly. Children had to face daily struggles that would put most modern adults under. Imagine sleeping rolled up in a buffalo hide, on frozen prairie ground, at twenty below zero. Then your mom chases you out of bed and tells you to gather lots of wood for the open fire. No matter how much you bring, most of the heat will go up the smoke-hole, and you will never be quite warm enough! And even though your dad's been gone four days and nights hunting, there's still no food. Your mom hopes he didn't get killed by enemies along the way. She boils you broth out of some old rawhide to keep you from starving.

Rugged outdoor life, simple and natural diet, hardiness from cold bathing, these things dictated life for children.

Today we can only look for aspects of such a life to try giving our children; it is no longer possible to raise them fully in such ways, even if we choose to try. But read them these stories, ask them if they would not like to go outdoors with you to experience a little something of what they hear about—parents and children just surviving in nature.

MY INDIAN GRANDMOTHER

As a motherless child, I always regarded my good grandmother as the wisest of guides and the best of protectors. . . .

I distinctly recall one occasion when she took me with her into the woods in search of certain medicinal roots.

"Why do you not use all kinds of roots for medicines?" said I.

"Because," she replied, in her quick, characteristic manner, "the Great Mystery does not will us to find things too easily. In that case everybody would be a medicine-giver, and Ohiyesa must learn that there are many secrets which the Great Mystery will disclose only to the most worthy. Only those who seek him fasting and in solitude will receive his signs."

With this and many similar explanations she wrought in my soul wonderful and lively conceptions of the "Great Mystery" and of the effects of prayer and solitude. I continued my childish questioning.

"But why did you not dig those plants that we saw in the woods, of the same kind that you are digging now?"

"For the same reason that we do not like the berries we find in the shadow of deep woods as well as the ones which grow in sunny places. The latter have more sweetness and flavor. Those herbs which have medicinal virtues should be sought in a place that is neither too wet nor too dry, and where they have a generous amount of sunshine to maintain their vigor.

(Excerpts from Charles Alexander Eastman, *Indian Boyhood,* McClure, Phillips & Co., New York, 1902)

"Someday Ohiyesa will be old enough to know the secrets of medicine; then I will tell him all. But if you should grow up to be a bad man, I must withhold these treasures from you and give them to your brother, for a medicine man must be a good and wise man. . . ."

She said these things so thoughtfully and impressively that I cannot but feel and remember them even to this day.

AN OMAHA BOY GETS NATIVE DOCTORING
by Francis La Flesche

[The following was witnessed by La Flesche during his tribal boyhood. One of his playmates was accidentally shot by another young fellow who, with some companions, was firing a pistol at a mark.]

After the shooting the excitement was so intense, and above all the noise could be heard the heartrending wails of the unfortunate man who had wounded the boy in the head. The relatives of the lad were preparing to avenge his death, and those of the man to defend him. I made my way through the crowd, and, peering over the shoulders of another boy, I saw on the ground the little form that I recognized. Blood was oozing from a wound in the back of the boy's head and from one under the right eye, near the nose. A man ordered the women to stop wailing and bade the people to stand back. Soon through an opening in the crowd I saw a tall man wrapped up in a buffalo robe come up the hill and pass through the space to where the boy lay. He stooped over the child, felt of his wrist,

---

(Excerpt from Alice C. Fletcher and Francis La Flesche, *The Omaha Tribe,* vol. 2, Twenty-seventh Annual Report of the Bureau of Ethnology, Smithsonian Institution, Washington, D.C., 1911)

and then of his heart. "He is alive," the man said; "set up a tent and take him in."

The little body was lifted on a robe and carried by two men into a large tent that had been hastily erected. Meanwhile a young man had been sent in all haste to call the buffalo doctors. Soon they were seen galloping over the hill on their horses, one or two at a time, their long hair flowing over their naked backs. They dismounted and one by one entered the tent, where they joined the buffalo doctor who lived nearby and had already been called. A short consultation was held. The sides of the tent were drawn up to let in the fresh air and to permit the people to witness the operation.

All the buffalo medicine men sat around the boy, their eyes gleaming over their wrinkled faces. Then one of the men began in a low voice to tell how in a vision he had seen the buffalo which had revealed to him the secret of the medicine and taught him the song he must sing when using it. At the end of every sentence the boy's father thanked him in terms of relationship. Then he compounded the roots he had taken from his skin pouch and started his song at the top of his voice. The other doctors, some twenty or more, joined in, and sang it in unison with a volume that could be heard a mile away. The song was accompanied by a bone whistle imitating the cry of the eagle. After the doctor had started the song he put the bits of roots into his mouth, ground them with his teeth, and taking a mouthful of water he approached the boy bellowing and pawing the earth like an angry buffalo at bay. When near the boy he drew in a long breath and with a whizzing noise forced the water from his mouth into the wound. The boy spread out his hands and winced as though he had been struck. The man uttered a series of short exclamations: "Hi! hi! hi!" Then the father and the man who had wounded the boy lifted their outspread hands toward the doctor to signify their thanks. During the administration of the medicine all the men and two women doctors sang with energy (a song) which had been started by the operator.

A second doctor now repeated the treatment and started his song, all the others joining in the singing as before, while he administered the remedy.

At the completion of the song a third doctor made ready to give his application. . . . [The story continues with each of the doctors taking a turn. One of the songs had words describing the doctoring of a wounded buffalo by its companions, at the edge of a pool of water. The buffalo were curing the wound with their saliva, and thus the native doctors were chewing up the herbs and spitting them into the boy's wound.]

The doctors remained all night, applying their medicine and dressing the wound. Four days the boy was treated in this manner. On the evening of the third day the doctors said the lad was out of danger, and that in the morning he would be made to stand and meet the rising sun, and so greet the return of life.

I went to bed early, so as to be up in time to see the ceremony. I was awakened by the sound of the singing, and hurried to the tent. Already a crowd had gathered. There was a mist in the air, as the doctors had foretold there would be, but as the dawn drew nearer the fog slowly disappeared, as if to unveil the great red sun that was just visible on the horizon. Slowly it grew larger and larger. The boy was gently lifted by two strong men, and when on his feet was told to take four steps toward the east, while the doctors sang the mystery song which belonged to this stage of the cure. The two men began to count as the boy feebly attempted to walk—one, two, three. The steps grew slower, and it did not seem as if he could make the fourth, but he dragged his foot and made the fourth. "Four!" cried the men; "it is done." Then the doctors sang the song of triumph.

The fees were then distributed. There were horses, robes, bear-claw necklaces, eagle feathers, embroidered leggings, and other articles of value. Toward these the relatives of the man, who shot the boy contributed largely. One or two doctors remained with the boy for a time. In a month or so he was back

among us, ready to play or to watch another pistol practice by
the young men.

A HIDATSA CHILDHOOD IN THE 1860s

When I was somewhat past ten years of age, my father took
me with him to watch the horses out on the prairie. We watered the herd and about the middle of the day came home for
dinner. In the afternoon we again took the herd out to graze.
There were many enemies around at the time and we had to
guard our horses closely.

While we sat watching the herd my father said: "These
horses are god[like], or mystery beings. They have supernatu-
ral power. If one cares for them properly and seeks good grazing and water for them, they will increase rapidly."

The boys of the household had a strange use for the first
dung dropped by a colt. It made an excellent yellow arrow
paint. We boys rubbed it on our arrowshafts, or sometimes
took it home and rubbed it on our playsticks, for the game
"umakiheke." This quality of the colt's dung continued for the
first two or three times a colt dunged. As I recollect it, we
picked the dung up in the morning and evening. It was a small,
gummy mass, about the size of one's thumb. We used it wet; or
if it was dry, we spat on it and rubbed the moistened part on
the arrowshaft.

My grandfather, Big-cloud, had a fine stallion named
Digs-out-dirt, because he always pawed up the dirt with his
hoofs when he came to a herd. He was often threatening to the
boy herders, putting his ears far back on his head and looking
savage, but he never really bit or harmed them. He was a good
stallion, forcing his attentions, in spite of avoidance and kicks.
He raised blue colts.

A colt was broken at two years of age, for a three-year-old

(Told by Wolf Chief in 1913 and 1918, excerpted from Gilbert L. Wilson, *The
Horse and the Dog in Hidatsa Culture,* American Museum Press, New York,
1924)

is nearly grown, and is then hard to break. Yearlings were sometimes broken but were apt to develop lameness, or grew knock-kneed from the weight of the boys riding them. The joints of a yearling's legs are still soft. Colts were broken by boys fourteen to seventeen years of age; but boys as young as eleven helped. As I have often broken colts, I will tell my own experience.

Several of us drove a herd down by the Missouri at a place where the current was rather swift, and so likely to prevent a swimming colt from getting back to shore too easily. I roped a two-year-old and drove him into deep water; swimming out to the colt, I mounted him and made him swim with me on his back. Now a two-year-old still suckles his mare, and frightened at my weight, the colt tried to make shore, where he knew his mare was. I clung to his back, forcing him to swim until, reaching shallow water, his feet touched ground, when he soon struggled to land. By this time I had dismounted. Following the colt, I drove him again into deep water and repeated the lesson; and so for two or three hours, until the colt was weary. The last time the colt came out, I stayed on his back.

Only one boy mounted a swimming colt, for under the weight of two a colt would sink. A horse drowns more easily than a man. "If a horse sinks until water runs into his ears, he grows weak," we Indians say.

As the colt reached shore the last time, another boy mounted behind me; and together we rode the poor beast back and forth over the low-lying sandbank covered with soft mud. . . . We rode the colt over such ground until it was utterly exhausted.

Had we tried to mount him when he was fresh, the colt would have bucked and very likely given us a fall. However, in the soft mud or in the sand we were not likely to be hurt even if we were thrown off; certainly, a fall here would not be as dangerous as on hard ground. It was usual for two boys to ride the colt we were breaking, as the animal was thus more rapidly exhausted. We always rode bareback when breaking a colt.

A colt was also taught to swim the Missouri. To train my

colt, I needed the help of two other boys. One of these swam ahead with a lariat, one end of which was bound about the colt's head like a halter. I followed, swimming on the down-stream side of the colt, guiding him, and clinging with one hand to his mane. A third boy swam at the colt's tail, but not grasping it; now and then he scratched the colt's ham or leg to frighten him and make him swim ahead.

I did not begin to train ponies for war until I was sixteen years old. A boy of fourteen we thought old enough to strike an enemy and some boys at this age began to train and manage war ponies. A boy as young as eleven might help break colts, but his legs were not strong enough for him to keep his seat on an untrained pony.

A war pony was trained to dance, as we called it. I took my previously broken two-year-old, mounted, and kicking him with my heels and drawing in my breath with a whistling sound through nearly closed lips, signaled him to go; but while doing thus, I also drew on my reins, jerking them repeatedly, as if to stop my pony. Not liking this, he tried to break away, but I checked him each time with the reins, and even struck him, not severely, on breast and fore legs, with my quirt. All this made the colt leap and prance about from side to side, his forelegs moving together, but his hind legs moving alternately.

I gave my colt several such lessons, in the morning and again in the evening. After two days, the pony had learned what was wanted of him.

Every war pony was taught to dance. In battle, unless a pony was constantly moving, he drew the enemy's fire upon horse and rider alike. . . .

On quiet evenings in summer, a young man painted and dressed in his best, often mounted his trained pony and paraded through the village, making the pony dance as he went. Usually just one young man paraded, not several in company; his purpose was to be admired by the village maidens. He wanted them to see what a fine figure he cut on his war pony. . . .

It was the duty of the boys of the household to herd the horses when they were grazing on the prairie or in the hills. We lads, as we guarded the herds, often hunted gophers or black-birds, which we cooked at a fire and ate. Sometimes we played the arrow-shooting game, two boys shooting against two others, or just one against another. The wager was often a bird or a gopher.

CHILDHOOD QUOTES

Sometimes for fun we lads used to take long poles with nooses on the end and snare off one ear of a braid of corn as it hung drying; for the braids were soft when fresh. An ear broken off, we would run and make a fire and parch the corn. This was when we were little fellows, ten or eleven years old. The owner would run after us, and if he caught one of us, whipped him. However, this was our custom; the owner and the boy's father looked upon it as a kind of lark, and not anything very serious.

EDWARD GOODBIRD

I do not think the younger Indians on this reservation are as good agriculturists as we older members of my tribe were when we were young. I sometimes say to my son Goodbird: "You young folks, when you want some green corn, open the husk to see if the grain is ripe enough, and thus expose it; but I just go out into the field and pluck the ear. When you open an ear and find it too green to pluck, you let it stand on the stalk; and birds then come and eat the exposed kernels, or little brown ants climb the stalk and eat the ear and spoil it."

BUFFALO-BIRD WOMAN

(Excerpt from Gilbert L. Wilson, *Agriculture of the Hidatsa Indians: An Indian Interpretation*, Univ. of Minnesota Studies in the Social Sciences, No. 9, 1977)

When I was six years old, there were, I think, ten in my father's family, of whom my two grandmothers, my mother and
her three sisters, made six. I have said that my mother and her
three sisters were wives of Small Ankle, my father.

My father's wives and my two grandmothers, all industrious women, added each year to the area of our field; for our
family was growing. At the time our garden reached its maxi-
mum size, there were seven boys in the family; three of these
died young, but four grew up and brought wives to live in our
earth lodge.

BUFFALO-BIRD WOMAN

When the squashes were brought in from the field, the little
girls would go to the pile and pick out squashes that were
proper for dolls. I have done so, myself. We used to pick out
the long ones that were parti-colored; squashes whose tops
were white or yellow and the bottoms of some other color. We
put no decorations on these squashes that we had for dolls.
Each little girl carried her squash about in her arms and sang
for it as for a babe. Often she carried it on her back, in her calfskin robe.

BUFFALO-BIRD WOMAN

My father, Small Ankle, liked to garden and often helped
his wives. He told me that that was the best way to do. "Whatever you do," he said, "help your wife in all things!" He taught
me to clean the garden, to help gather the corn, to hoe, and to
rake.

In my tribe in old times, some men helped their wives in
the gardens, others did not. Those who did not ... talked
against those who did, saying, "That man's wife makes him her
servant."

And others retorted, "Look, that man puts all the hard
work on his wife!"

My father said that that man lived best and had plenty to

eat who helped his wife. One who did not help his wife was
likely to have scanty stores of food.

WOLF CHIEF

The first pots, or kettles, of metal that we Hidatsas got were
of yellow tin [brass]; the French and the Crees also traded us
kettles made of red tin [copper].

As long as we could get our native clay pots, we of my father's family did not use metal pots much, because the metal
made the food taste. When I was a little girl, if any of us went
to visit another family, and they gave us food cooked in an iron
pot, we knew it at once because we could taste and smell the
iron in the food.

BUFFALO-BIRD WOMAN

Tobacco was cultivated in my tribe only by old men. Our
young men did not smoke much; a few did, but most of them
used little tobacco, or almost none. They were taught that
smoking would injure their lungs and make them short-winded
so that they would be poor runners. But when a man got to be
about sixty years of age we thought it right for him to smoke as
much as he liked. His war days and hunting days were over.
Old men smoked quite a good deal.

BUFFALO-BIRD WOMAN

GOODBIRD IS NEARLY DROWNED

At the mouth of the Little Missouri River, we almost had a
fatal accident. When we left our winter camp in the west [in the
spring of 1869], the grass was growing and the snow had disappeared, but as we came down the Missouri, a snowstorm

---

(Told by his mother, Buffalo-bird Woman, a Hidatsa, excerpted from Gilbert L.
Wilson, *The Horse and the Dog in Hidatsa Culture,* American Museum Press,
New York, 1924)

came up very suddenly. A strong wind blew; as we rounded the bend at the Little Missouri River, the water was very rough and the waves tossed our boats around so that we were all frightened. Of course, we turned toward shore, both my husband and I paddling vigorously. Usually, in paddling a bullboat [a round, dish-like craft made of willow framing covered by buffalo-bull hides], when a husband and wife are together, the wife kneels in front and paddles while the husband sits in the tail of the boat to balance it.

Coming down the Missouri, towing a load, was a more difficult operation, so both my husband and I paddled side by side in the boat. Suddenly, my husband stopped paddling and leaned over the side of the boat so far that I was nearly pitched over on his side. A bull-boat is a clumsy, tub-like craft, easily upset. My husband leaned over so far that the edge of the boat came clear down on his stomach. "He has dropped the child," I heard him cry, and saw him lift my baby into the boat. "Ina," I cried, but I had presence of mind enough not to drop my paddle. Indeed, we could not have reached shore without our paddles.

As I have already explained, Flies-low, my younger brother, was in the second boat, holding my son, Goodbird. It was customary when a young child cried, to loosen his cradle clothes. After my husband drew the child into the boat, I found that Goodbird's clothes had been so treated. Probably the child had become restless and Flies-low had loosened his clothes a little to give him room to move his limbs. This loosening of the cradle wrapping had made them buoyant, so that the baby floated on the water and my husband was able to rescue him.

We came ashore without any further mishap and camped in two tents. It began to rain, then the weather turned colder and a heavy snow began to fall and continued for four days. Many of the summer birds had already come north and when the storm was over we found some of them frozen to death.

Goodbird was crying lustily when we drew him out of the water, but was not choking or strangling. I do not think that his

Left, a baby of the Umatilla tribe of Oregon, in the early 1900s, looking quite content in its attractive little "shell." The basic cradleboard is of flat wood, covered by soft paddings and cloths, then wrapped by a dark velvet cover, which is decorated with floral beadwork, cloth edging, and ornate borders of small brass discs sewn all around. The "headband" appears to be an adult's dentalium-shell choker, used here just for the photograph, along with the double strand of shell beads. *Below,* this mounted Salish-Flathead girl was dressed for a tribal parade in Western Montana, about 1907. She is riding a traditional "woman's saddle," such as might have been used daily in prereservation years. Its conspicuous features are the high, beaded pommels and large bead-covered stirrups. She is wearing a shell-decorated dress and is wrapped in a tanned elk robe that would have been worn in the "old days" in lieu of sweaters, coats, and blankets. The long-fringed bag, which hangs down behind her on both sides, was used as a combination purse and overnight suitcase back when this girl's people often had their main belongings packed and on the move. Only, then there would not have been as much beadwork on the horse—at least not for everyday use.

Recalling how it was in *his* young days. A Blackfeet grandfather shows his little schoolboy grandson a miniature painted tipi of the kind he grew up in. While missionary schools often forbade all signs of native culture, government schools sometimes sponsored fairs that included craftwork displays like this one, along with powwow dances and storytelling sessions.

Mary Ann Combs (*left*) with her family soon after they sadly followed Chief Charlo away from the Flathead ancestral lands in Western Montana, during the 1890s. In her old age she became the last woman on the Flathead reservation who was initiated as a young girl into a traditional and disciplined tribal life. Here she is seen with her mother; younger brother, Pete; father, Louis Pierre; and her sister.

Although not far removed from their ancestral past, these boys appear to be far from it in their daily lives. This 1930s scene shows a Jesuit mission school in Desmet, Idaho. There is no explanation on the photograph for the fact that the two boys are wearing headdresses, though the horned item is only a poor imitation of such a style and may have been made for the priest's "souvenier" collection.

This Catholic nun believed that her duty was to teach these Indian children to grow up like white children so they might be saved from the pagan sufferings of their parents and grandparents. Such attitudes continued in many Indian schools into the 1950s, although now they are about all gone. This photograph was taken in the 1920s at St. Mary's Indian Boarding School, on the Blood Reserve of Alberta, Canada, where both Beverly and her parents received schooling.

Piegan-Blackfeet girl of Western Montana in front of her own small tipi. Parents who could afford the added work and expense provided miniature tipis in which their children could entertain friends. Among the Blackfeet certain children were especially honored by getting one of the sacred tipi designs ritually transferred to them. Paula Weaselhead, long an elder in our family, got lifelong spiritual benefits from such a painted tipi ceremonial, which she went through as a small girl, around 1910. This girl is wearing a buckskin dress decorated at the top with rows of beadwork alternated with cowrie shells, plus many strings of fringes, some with beads on them.

Above, Alberta Indian boys from various tribes are seen racing their horses at the world-famous Calgary Stampede, in the 1920s. Many Indian children have been able to experience some of their ancestral outdoor life right up to the present day by growing up among horses, one reason for the popularity of rodeos among native youths. Note that several boys are wearing scarves on their heads, a common practice for native men who lived in windy places.

Left, Kiowa parents and their little daughter, wearing traditional dress, somewhere in Oklahoma during the 1920s. The children of most Plains tribes wore long hair that was braided as soon as it was long enough. Before then, some children wore bangs, and others had a little topknot, like this one, to keep the hair from the forehead. In some sacred ceremonies such topknots became the centers of ritual initiation.

A father-and-son dancing team—Jim White Grass and his boy—of the Blackfeet in Montana, as they looked in 1927. Many Indian boys of this era grew up in households where traditional culture was practiced daily, so even while they became successful ranchers and farmers, they harbored a deep love and longing for the culture. In their old age, some have become teachers and elders to the many youths interested in native cultural revival since the 1960s. The trend has brought many an elderly Indian back to the cultural roots of childhood after years of living like "white men."

Beaverhead, a noted Flathead warrior and dancer, with his "little girl," in 1910. The man had several children of which this one was a favorite. The family spent winters in a log cabin and summers outdoors, using tipis.

A quiet afternoon in the tribal camp. Our oldest boy, Wolf, seemed to be contemplating his carefree life outdoors on the Southern Alberta prairie in 1974. Many old Indians have told us their favorite memories are of childhood camping days.

Left, Blackfeet boy in a contemporary dance costume of the 1930s, seen at Glacier National Park. The decline in such traditional crafts as hide tanning and beadwork was evidenced in costumes like this, made mostly from store-bought materials. It was a practical answer for parents of children who spent most of each year in schools, with little time to wear tribal clothing that requires weeks and months to prepare.

Calvin Boy was among the last Blackfeet children of Montana to be raised in traditional households of old warriors and buffalo hunters, such as his grandfather, Bird Rattler. His stepfather was Theodore Last Star, recognized by many as a tribal chief, who brought the boy to many ceremonials and dances. His Indian name, Flying Higher, foretold future accomplishments, including those as published artist. His passing at middle age was a loss for Blackfeet culture. The photo shows him in 1938 wearing his handmade costume.

The old way of transporting Indian children across the Plains! This Blackfoot grandmother was photographed about 1915, dressed up for a tribal parade within the tipi encampment. The children are sitting on top of the woman's household goods, including folded buffalo robes and flat rawhide containers called parfleches. Backrests made of willow sticks are seen dangling down behind. The whole works is tied to an A-framed travois, the tops of which the woman is straddling. Legends recall some occasions when kids fell off these moving seats and were lost during tribal movements, though usually everyone worked together to watch for such mishaps.

Left, Maxi-diwiac, or Buffalo-bird Woman, wise elder of the Hidatsa tribe in 1910. From her came many fascinating accounts of native childhood life in the mid-1800s, when she was the respectable daughter of the tribe's chief. She spoke no English, and practiced her native ways right to the end, but she eagerly contributed to the ethnological works being published by Dr. Gilbert L. Wilson, whose sincere interest caused her to adopt him as a son.

A special child, or *minipoka,* of the Siksika, or Canadian Blackfoot. To bestow honor and blessings on their son, his parents have just had an old warrior give him an ancient war shield, hanging from his back. The transfer ritual included songs, prayers, and body paintings, through which the boy could learn to depend on the shield's mystical powers as he grew older. In the buffalo days he would have been expected to become a leading warrior. But the poor lad faced changing times by 1910 or so, when this picture was taken. Occasions where a grown man could walk around with a feather-decorated shield on his back were limited to parades and Wild West shows. This shield ended up in a museum collection, and when the fellow passed away, he took its mystical initiations with him. Each of the two white shells on necklaces indicates a ritual initiation to the mysteries of some Medicine Pipe Bundle.

Kutenai Indian twins, Elizabeth and Mary, daughters of Ambrose and Cecile Gravelle, sleeping in bead-covered cradleboards. In many tribes it was thought to be a special blessing for parents to have twins, while in a few it was considered a curse. Some traditions even required twins to be separated and one disposed of. There seem to be no recollections of Indian mothers giving birth to more than twins, and the rugged life-styles of the past would have made survival difficult for weak and competing babies, as with most large mammals in nature.

A Blackfoot father and his beloved son, ready to enter the sacred Sun Dance Lodge, or Okan, one summer in the 1890s. The man is dressed as for the warpath, wearing leggings and capote made of Hudson's Bay Company striped blankets and carrying his carbine. Inside the sacred lodge he would be joining his lifelong comrades, the members of one of several Blackfoot warrior societies. As part of the four-day celebrations and ceremonials, they would help each other reenact the bravest deeds of their lives. Because of the people's total commitment to Sun and Nature, only *real* incidents were portrayed, in honest ways. The whole exercise was a form of confession, at the same time dramatizing the tribe's most important events for the benefit of all the watching members. . . . For the boy on the horse, this event was probably the highlight of his year. The decorated horse was going to represent some important animal during one of the deed recountings; likely his father made a present of it to someone in the crowd whom he wanted to honor. If he was really lucky, the boy might even have been allowed to play an enemy who was overpowered while on a horse. He would have gotten some feeling of how his dad's best friends looked and acted when they fought to the death with enemies. Even inside the sacred lodge they would be shooting their rifles into the air and behaving wildly. The quiet and sacred parts of the Sun Dance are always completed before this historic dramatizing begins.

Children from tribes near the Canadian Rockies are seen in dance costumes at a special powwow with parents in Banff National Park in 1962. Because tourists paid to watch the dancing, some have criticized such events as "stage shows." Yet participants have generally voiced satisfaction, saying they don't mind being watched by strangers who like to see what *they* enjoy doing! Such dances have helped many Indian children retain something of their own cultures.

Beverly's grandmother, Hilda Strangling Wolf, showing the most common Blackfoot way of carrying little children around. When this is properly done, it causes limited strain on the mother's back, even while she is working, and lets the child ride safely, comfortably, and securely. When this photo was taken in the 1930s, Grandma Ana-daki wore blankets and shawls much of the time anyway. By the 1980s, when she was getting close to one hundred, things had changed so that her grandchildren were frequently carrying her around!

face got into the water at all. I do not remember now whether Flies-low made any outcry when he dropped the infant into the river or not. I did not scold Flies-low. "I am not to blame," he said. "I tried to hold the baby, but that boat seemed to turn upside down and the baby fell out of my arms."

THE PAWNEE GIRL WHO SAVED A PRISONER

The Pawnee had set out on one of their summer buffalo hunts. Only a few old and sickly people remained in the villages. On the third day of their march they reached the Loupe [River]. The main body crossed and pitched camp among the hills, but far behind were a few stragglers and a group of boys playing the hoop game. The latter stopped at the river to finish a game before crossing. Here they were discovered by a Dakota war party and surprised. They scattered out for cover, but a few got away with their horses and crossing the river fled toward the camp of the main body. The whole Dakota party crossed in hot pursuit and were thus led into a trap, for the Pawnee in camp had seen the signals and the whole armed body dashed to the rescue. Many of the Dakota were killed in the running fight that followed.

When the pursuing Pawnee returned they went over the field to count the dead and collect the spoils. As they were going along one of the Dakota arose and looked in a bewildered manner; he had only been stunned by the fall of his horse. He was seized and taken to camp. According to custom he was taken to the chief for instructions. He consulted with the society of braves, then in charge of the camp, and it was decided to turn him over to the women's society. A messenger was sent to inform the leader of this organization. She at once

(Excerpt from James R. Murie, *Pawnee Indian Societies,* American Museum of Natural History, New York, 1914)

called in the members, who proceeded to the chief's tipi, marched the prisoner out to the south of the camp where they bound him to a tree.

The women then returned to the lodge of their leader to prepare their regalia. When all was ready they danced through the village and paraded to the place of torture. Then, as was the custom, they kindled a large fire in front of the prisoner and prepared for a four-day ceremony. Every indignity was offered the unfortunate prisoner. Old women would urinate in bowls and force him to drink. Others would take up coals of fire and touch him here and there.

On the third day the chief's wife took her little girl out to see the tortures. While they were there an old woman came up with a bundle. She took out a large piece of dried back fat. This she heated in the fire until hot and while other women held the prisoner she spread it on his back. The little girl was overcome at the sight and began to scream. Her mother took her home but she cried and refused to be comforted. Finally, the chief asked the cause of this crying and was informed. He coaxed and threatened without result for the child declared that she would continue to scream until the prisoner was turned loose. The chief said that could not be done and so the child continued to wail. The people gathered in and gradually developed sympathy for the child. So the chief called in the braves, but they declared themselves powerless. Then he called in the chiefs and the soldiers to discuss the matter. The sentiment of the camp was now aroused, so four soldiers were sent out to order the women's society to disband. They then conducted the prisoner to the council lodge and seated him there.

The chief then sent for his daughter, who had stopped crying. He stated that they had with some difficulty granted her wish and that now she must get water for the prisoner. Accordingly she brought water and held the bowl for him to drink. Then the chief ordered her to get a large bowl of water and some buffalo wool and when these were brought to wash the man's wounds. Then buffalo fat mixed with red earth was given her to rub over him.

Now, said the chief, since you would have this man released, you must feed him. So dried meat and fat were brought. Some of the fat she handed to the man to eat, while she cooked the dried meat. When ready she set the food before him, placed four small bits of meat in his mouth and then signed for him to eat. When he had finished, she set a bowl of water for him to wash. The chief then gave her permission to withdraw.

Then the chief sent for his horses. He ordered his best horse prepared for riding and loaded with baggage for the journey. Next he brought out clothing and dressed the man in his own fine clothes, even his ceremonial leggings, shirt, and moccasins. Finally, the girl brought a new robe and wrapped it around the man. The chief then addressed the Dakota: "You are to go home. You are a free man. All these things we give you. My daughter here saved your life. She alone did it. Now go to your people and tell them of her deeds."

Some three years later the Pawnee were surprised to receive a visit from their enemies, the Dakota. It was a very large party that came to the chief's lodge. The leader asked for the girl who saved the life of a Dakota. Then they knew him. The chief took him into his own lodge and the others were quartered in the village.

The Pawnee entertained their guests well. On the last day they gave the Iruska dance for their visitors. The Dakota entered into the dance. He was naked; on his body were painted red spots to show his burns and many prints of hands since he had been held by many of the Pawnee. He addressed the Pawnee, explaining that he had come to see his daughter once more, she who had saved his life, that his own people did not believe his story; hence he brought them that they might see for themselves. In return the Pawnee vouched for the narrative.

Many times during his life this Dakota visited the Pawnee and he labored unceasingly to bring about a permanent peace between them and his people.

RIDING A DOG TRAVOIS

Small boys sometimes jumped on a dog travois just for the fun of it. Once I asked my husband to go for wood with me to the timber east of the village. I had three dogs and travois. My son, Goodbird, who was then four or five years old, wanted to go along. My husband and I said, "No, you cannot go." Goodbird wept and wept, so at last we took him with us. As we went along, my little son jumped on and off the travois, walking and riding, and playing with the dogs. The dogs got into a fight and ran off with my little son. He was much frightened and we laugh about it to this day.

BUFFALO-BIRD WOMAN

I remember that. There was a road down to the timber and another road that led to the chokecherry hills crossed it. We were going along the latter, my father and mother walking ahead, when a woman came down the first road on her way to the village. She had two or three dogs with travois. Our dogs saw the others and started across the triangle that lay between the two roads. The other dogs also turned toward ours barking. I yelled, "Ai, ai, ai!" I was dreadfully frightened; the dogs were leaping along at such a rate that I was afraid to jump off. The other woman ran between the dogs with her arms up in the air. "Na! na!" she cried. "Go away! Go away!" That stopped our dogs. I jumped off the travois and ran to my mother. I did not want to ride on that travois again!

GOODBIRD

(Excerpt from Gilbert L. Wilson, *The Horse and the Dog in Hidatsa Culture*, American Museum Press, New York, 1924)

GAMES PLAYED BY OMAHA CHILDREN

In their play the children were apt to mimic the occupations of their elders. At an early age the girls began to play "keep house." Miniature tents were set up. The mother's robe or shawl was often seized for a tent cover; the poles were frequently tall sunflower stalks. If the boys were gallant, they would cut the poles for the girls. It was a matter of delight if the tent was large enough to creep into. Generally the feet and legs would protrude but if the heads were well under cover it was easy to "make-believe."

Both boys and girls liked to play "going on the hunt." The boys took two parts—they were hunters sometimes and sometimes ponies. When the latter, the girls tied the tent cover in a bundle and fastened it and the tent poles to the boy pony, who might be a docile creature or a very fractious animal.... Sometimes men carried through life their pony reputation. Women would laughingly point out some elderly man and say: "He used to be a very bad pony," or else "a very good pony."

The boys who played warrior wore war bonnets made from corn husks, which cost much labor to manufacture and were quite effective when well done. Children made many of their playthings out of clay and some were very clever in modeling dishes, pipes, dolls, tents, etc....

Dolls were improvised by children from corncobs. Sometimes mothers made dolls for their little girls and also small dishes....

The hobby-horse of the boys was a sunflower stalk with one nodding bloom left on the end. Races were run on these "make-believe" ponies. Generally the boys rode one stalk and trailed two or three others as "fresh horses."

(Excerpt from Alice C. Fletcher and Francis La Flesche, *The Omaha Tribe,* vol. 2, Twenty-seventh Annual Report of the Bureau of American Ethnology, Smithsonian Institution, Washington, D.C., 1911)

"The crooked path" was the game familiarly known to us as "follow my leader." The children sang as they ran and made their merry way through the village, each one repeating the pranks of the leader. The line was kept by each boy holding to the string about the waist of the boy in front. It is said that the song which accompanied this game had been handed down by generations of children. Certainly every Omaha seemed to know it.

The quiet games often played about the fire were "cat's cradle" [in Omaha called "the litter"] and a game resembling jackstraws, in which a bunch of joints of prairie grass was dropped from one's hand and the players strove to pull out one joint after another without disturbing the bunch. The player could use a joint to disentangle those he was trying to secure.

Another game, called "dua," was played with a long stick one side of which was notched. The person who could touch the greatest number of notches, saying "dua" at every notch without taking a breath, was winner.

The boys enjoyed a game called "bone slide." Formerly ribs were used; sticks are now substituted. Four or five could play at this game. The sticks are about 4½ feet long, made of red willow, and ornamented by banding with bark and then holding them over a fire. The exposed part turns brown and when the bands are removed the sticks are striped brown and white. Each boy holds a number of sticks and throws one so it will skim or slide along the level ground or the ice. The boy who throws his sticks farthest wins all the sticks; the one who loses is tapped on the head by the winner. The Ponca call this game "arrow throwing."

During the annual buffalo hunt when the tribe remained in a camp for more than a day the boys, ranging from ten to fourteen years of age, would ... arm themselves with sticks about a yard long, to which small twigs were attached; then ranging in line through the prairie grass they scared up the little birds. As these rose, the boys threw their sticks into the air and the fledglings, mistaking them for hawks, tumbled into the grass to hide, only to be caught by the hands of the boys. One lad was chosen to carry the quarry. As soon as the bird was caught, it was killed, scalped, and thrown at the boy appointed to take charge of the game; then it was his duty to run ahead and fall into the grass as if shot. On rising, he took the bird and strung it on his bow string. This little pantomime was enacted with every bird caught. When a number of birds had been captured, the boys retired to a place where they could roast the birds and enjoy a feast. Boys of [certain] gens [or clans] could join in the sport but could not touch the birds or share in the feast, as small birds were tabu to them.

In winter the boys played whip top. They made their own tops out of wood. Sometimes a round-pointed stone served as a top, and was spun on the smooth ice.

A ball game called "ball, to toss by striking," which resembles somewhat the game known as shinny, was played by two groups, or parties. This is the game ... sometimes played between the two divisions of the [Omaha] tribe, which had a cosmic significance in reference to the winds and the earth. ...

Two stakes, as goals for the two sides, were set at a considerable distance apart. The players with the ball started from the center. The aim of each player was to drive the ball to the goal of his side, while the players on the opposing side tried to prevent this and to drive the ball to their own goal. The bat used was a stick crooked at one end.

When boy neighbors played together, the "sides" were chosen in the following manner: A boy was selected to choose the sticks. He took a seat on the ground and another boy stood behind him. The standing boy held his hands over the eyes of the seated boy. Then all the sticks were laid in a pile before the latter. He took two sticks, felt them, trying to recognize to what boy they belonged. Then he crossed his hands and laid one stick on one side and the other on the other side of the place where he was sitting. When all the sticks had been taken up and laid on one or the other pile, the standing boy removed his hands and the boy who had chosen sticks indicated to which pile or side he would belong. There were no leaders in the game—the ball was tossed and the sides fell to playing. When men played this game, large stakes were often put up, as gar-ments, robes, horses, bows and arrows, and guns. No stakes were ventured when boys were the players.

Lads sometimes indulged in a game ... which may be called "dare," consisting of lads doing ridiculous things, which required exertion to accomplish. Some of the number were de-tailed to see that the boys actually did the things called for. Many are the laughs the older men have over these "hazing" sports of their youth, as they recount their escapades.

Girls had a game ... played with two balls tied together and a stick (the obvious symbolism was an accepted part of the game among all the tribes who played it). Two goals were set up several yards apart. The players were divided into two par-ties, each with its goal. They started in the middle and each side tried to prevent the other's balls from reaching the goal.

Foot racing was another pastime. Races generally took place among the Omaha, however, after a death, when gifts contributed by the family of the deceased youth or maiden were distributed among the successful competitors. At these races sharp contrasts marked the occasion. The race generally took place a short time after the burial. A feast was given by the parents, after which if the deceased was a young man his young men friends took part in the race; if a girl, her young companions competed for her possessions. The distribution of the goods was made by a personal friend, while the parents often retired to the grave, where the sound of their wailing could be heard above the noise of the contestants.

There was one amusement in which both sexes of all ages, except infants, took great pleasure; this was swimming. The Omaha swam by treading, moving hands and legs like a dog, or by keeping the body horizontal and throwing the arms up and out of the water alternately as the body was propelled by the legs. The people were good swimmers. The current in the Missouri is always strong, so that it requires a good swimmer to

make a safe passage across the stream. During the flood season
the current is too rapid for anyone to venture to cross the river.
Diving was practiced by boys and girls and was enjoyed by
men and women also. In these water sports the sexes did not
mingle; women and girls kept together and apart from the men
and boys (this was the case among most, though not all, tribes).

Story telling was the delight of everyone during the winter
evenings. It was then that the old folk drew on their store of
memories, and myths, fables, the adventures of the pygmies
and of the "gajazhe" [the little people who play about the
woods and prairies and lead people astray]—all these and also
actual occurrences were recited with varying intonation and il-
lustrative gesture, sometimes interspersed with song, which
added to the effect and heightened the spell of the story or
myth over the listeners clustered about the blazing fire.

The uncle [the mother's brother], who was always a privileged character and at whose practical jokes no nephew or
niece must ever take offense, often made the evening merry
with pranks of all sorts, from the casting of shadow pictures on
the wall with his fingers to improvising dances and various
rompings with the little ones.

In the spring, after the thunder had sounded, the boys had
a festivity called [striped face], referring to the mask worn by
the boys. A dried [buffalo] bladder, with holes cut for the
mouth and eyes, was pulled over the head; the bladder was
striped lengthwise in black and white, to represent lightning.
The boys carried clubs and scattered over the village. Each boy
went to the tent of his uncle [his mother's brother] and beat
with his club against the tent pole at the door, while he made a
growling sound in imitation of thunder. The uncle called out,
"What does Striped Face want?" The boy disguised his voice,
and said, "I want leggings or moccasins or some other article."
Then the uncle called him in and made him a present. Should
the uncle refuse to give anything the boy might punch a hole in
the tent or do some other mischief. But generally the sport
ended pleasantly and was greatly enjoyed by old and young.

A TAOS SCHOOLBOY AT
HOME FOR THE SUMMER

Summer passed slowly in Taos. There were long days and happy star-lit nights.

There were days of irrigating. The boys turned the slow-moving water from Mother-ditch into the little ditches to feed the thirsty plants of fields and gardens.

Pachole always was patient. He never grew tired of waiting until each plant had its share to drink. He taught Tso'u to think long thoughts while the lazy water moved along, wetting the thirsty earth.

There were days and days of wood gathering. Out-of-door ovens are greedy for the dry branches of the mountain slopes.

Pachole taught Tso'u how to tie the sticks into bundles that fit the back with comfort. He taught him how to save his breath in the high places, how to breathe in climbing upward, how to bend his knees in walking down hill. He showed his smaller brother how feet must keep their balance when walking over rolling stones.

The boys dug yucca weed for its fibers. They dug its root for soap. They gathered wild tea and guaco and juniper berries for their mothers to use. They rubbed their faces with the leaves of aspen to keep the wind and sun from burning them. Tso'u helped Iao to dry rose petals. All Taos girls have pillows stuffed with dried rose petals.

Pachole showed Tso'u the plants that were used for snake bite and for medicines. Pachole knew them all. He was rich in learning.

The boys found the tracks of mountain lion and wildcat. They found a packrat's nest with its sweet little pinon nuts. One noon they rested at the bedded-down place of a bear and her cubs. They saw the deep scratchings high up on the trunk

(Excerpt from Ann Clark, *Little Boy with Three Names,* Bureau of Indian Affairs, Chilocco, Oklahoma, 1940)

of a near-by pine tree where the mother bear had sharpened her great claws. They touched the lower scratchings on the pine tree where the bear cubs had sharpened their little claws.

Once they saw a deer looking at them through the aspen trees. They smoked a prairie dog family out of its underground hole. They saw an owl on a tree. They shot a chicken hawk, flying.

Pachole taught Tso'u how to use his gun. He taught him how to oil and clean it. Father promised that next summer Tso'u should own a gun.

At night Pachole would point out the evening star. He would join in the evening dancing. The old men would listen and nod. Their choice had been wise. They were pleased.

The winds and the shadows, the moon and the stars, were as books to Pachole. He was being taught to read them.

The long days of summer moved slowly.

In the early mornings all the boys of the village ran races. Sometimes they ran in great numbers. Other times they ran in small groups of three and four. They liked racing.

Tso'u was a swift runner. Pachole could teach him little about running. He ran swiftly and lightly like a young antelope. His feet scarcely touched the ground. "I win all the races," he told his mother. "It is because of the moccasins of deerskin which you made for me. I am a great runner among the boys."

His mother was not pleased with him. "Spend your time in thanking your moccasins," she told him, "and not in bragging."

Tso'u went out and sat upon the ladder of his mother's house. He was sorry that his mother had found it wise to scold him.

In the evenings the people danced. In the houses and in the plaza they danced. Sometimes the women and girls did the circle dance or the scalp dance or did dances borrowed from the Plains Indians. The men gathered around them and sang and beat the drum.

Sometimes the men and boys danced. They danced the fun dances and the dances of the summer season.

Old men taught the young boys the right steps and the words of the songs. Tso'u and Pachole learned the hoop dance. Uncle sang for them. Over and over they did the hoop dance, for the people liked to watch them.

When the moon was high the young men gathered at the little river which ran through the plaza. The young men of the south plaza stood on the south bank of the little river. The young men of the north plaza stood on the north bank of the little river. They joined their singing. They sang love songs to the girls of the village. They wrapped themselves in their white sheets and sang songs in Taos and in English. They made the music for their singing with their drums.

Sometimes Tso'u and Pachole went with the young men to the little river. They sat on the bridge with the other boys. They must know all the songs when their time came for singing. They wrapped their white sheets about them and learned the words and the music.

CHAPTER FIVE

Finding a Mate

Boys and girls of the tribal days were often paired up by their parents while still very young. Though this custom may seem rather arbitrary by our modern standards, it generally led to successful marriages, which is more than can often be said today. Of course, back then everyone in the tribe shared the same basic goals and aspirations; tribal customs dictated the ways of life, which left little for husbands and wives to disagree about, especially in comparison with the lack of standards these days.

Indian children had a lot more freedom in their younger years than modern kids, but once those times were over, they went right into serious adulthood. In tribal camps there was not really a place for teenage life as such. Girls in their teen years usually got married, boys did the hunting and fought with enemies, along with the men. Of course, nowadays teenagers are as conspicuous a group within Indian tribes as in any other social group.

One old woman we knew got married when she was only seven! Teenage life for her was a time of having children, being a woman, no parties or boyfriends. We know an old man from the same tribe who got married when he was twelve, though he was the only one in his age group who had a wife. He said his friends teased him about it, especially since the wife was younger and still played with dolls.

Both of these old people had long and prosperous lives with their childhood partners, and both spoke about the need for discipline within the marriage and the family in terms of fulfilling commitments. In their young days, single parents were almost unknown.

It is a sign of leisure in our own society that we can afford to let our children be teenagers for several years. The reality of daily wilderness life required that everyone in the tribe do whatever work he or she was capable of. Food was of primary concern, so in large families children were often encouraged to marry early so that they could provide their own. This was especially true if there were several girls in a household. Boys were at least able to hunt and thus contribute to the larder.

Parents generally had a hand in picking mates for their children for several reasons. If their child was a girl, they wanted a son-in-law who would treat her kindly, and also one who would treat them kindly, supplying them with meat and horses if they should need it. Some well-off parents wanted their kids to marry into families like theirs, to ensure continued ambition. Or rich parents of a girl might select, instead, a very poor boy—even an orphan—who would then be available to take care of their horses, as well as their food needs. Lazy, dirty, or mean kids usually ended up being mates to each other, since all the "good ones" would be accounted for. In the case of girls, they might instead become the second or third wife of a successful man, whose family put up with her in return for making her do much of the work. Lazy boys sometimes had to go out and steal a wife from the enemy if no decent girl would have them.

Young girls were often given away for marriage by their parents while quite young in order to preserve their virginity. Although virginity was often a high tribal virtue, people recog-

nized that girls within such closed societies were under growing pressure to mate with the men around them. Those who
were strong enough to resist all temptations were eligible in
some tribes for the very highest honor, involving sacred ceremonies for the Sun. Such women have always been few in
number, but there are yet a few tribes who have them.

In recent times there has been a lot of interest shown in
"traditional Indian marriages," which are often very colorful
and inspiring ceremonies. But very few tribes actually had anything like the marriage ceremonies we envision. Generally two
people became husband and wife after sharing a bed together.
The parents might make a big ritual out of exchanging valuable presents, but this had little to do with the couple themselves. They didn't usually stand shyly in the camp circle
holding hands while everyone threw dried berries. Rather, they
carried on with their normal, daily chores, and that night they
slept together. If all was well, they got their own tipi or lodge.
Often as not one moved in with the other, *and* that one's
family!

If there was a ceremony at all, its major significance was the
"coming of age." From being mere children, the husband and
wife suddenly had all the responsibilities of grown-ups. They
then went through a period of trial and error, through which,
however, most survived. If the mating didn't work out, the two
went back to their respective homes and waited for another try,
usually with someone else. In the traditional tribal camps it
was practically a foregone conclusion that males and females
would mate together, and the emphasis was on becoming
mates for life.

It should be pointed out that many young people *did* marry
the mates of their choice, even if not always with the support of
their parents. Boys, especially, were often allowed to select a
potential wife, whose parents were then approached by a relative or friend bearing gifts with the request. If the girl's parents
were kind people, they would ask her opinion on the matter; if
not, they would accept or reject the boy based on their own

judgment. There were no firm rules about this, each family deciding how to handle the marriage their own way, except, again, that tribal custom decreed that two mates sleeping together were automatically husband and wife.

OMAHA MARRIAGE CUSTOMS

When a young man asked the hand of a girl in marriage he observed a certain conventional form of address. The words were not always the same, but the aspect put on the proposal was practically uniform. The young man extolled the girl and her relations; he did not vaunt himself; he pleaded his constancy and asked, rather than demanded, that she become his wife, craving it as a boon. There were signals other than songs or flute calls to let a girl know her lover was near. A tent pole might fall or some other noise be made which she would know how to interpret and so be able to meet the young man if a meeting had been agreed on.

Marriage was usually by elopement. The claims on a girl [by those] holding a potential right to marry her almost necessitated her escaping secretly if she would exercise her free choice in the matter of a husband. When a young couple during their courtship determined on taking the final step of marriage, they agreed to meet some evening. The youth generally rode to a place near the lodge of the girl and gave the proper signal; she stepped out and they galloped off to one of his relations. In a day or two the young man took the girl to his father's lodge where, if she was received as his wife, all claims by other men as to marriage were cancelled by this act, but gifts had to be made to the girl's parents and shared with her relatives, in order to ratify the marriage.

To bring this about, the father of the young man made a

(Excerpt from Alice C. Fletcher and Francis La Flesche, *The Omaha Tribe,* vol. 2, Twenty-seventh Annual Report of the Bureau of American Ethnology, Smithsonian Institution, Washington, D.C., 1911)

feast and invited the relatives of the girl. When this invitation was accepted and the presents received, the marriage was considered as settled beyond all dispute. In the course of a few months the father of the bride generally presented his daughter with return gifts about equal in value to those he had received and the young husband was expected to work for a year or two for his father-in-law. This latter claim was frequently rigidly exacted and the father-in-law was sometimes a tyrant over his son-in-law's affairs.

Men and women were socially on a moral equality. Tribal custom favored chastity and those who practiced it stood higher in public esteem than those who did not. In the case of a woman who in her youth committed indiscretions and later led a moral life, while her former acts were remembered, they were not held against her or her husband or children. Both men and women were allowed to win back by subsequent good conduct their past position.

Cohabitation constituted marriage whether the relationship was of long or short duration, always provided that the woman was not the wife of another man, in which case the relationship was a social and punishable offense. Prostitution, as practiced in a white community, did not exist in the tribe.

In the family the father was recognized as having the highest authority over all the members, although in most matters pertaining to the welfare of the children the mother exercised almost equal authority. . . . During the lifetime of the parents the uncle was as alert as their father to defend the children or to avenge a wrong done them. The children always regarded their uncle as their friend, ever ready to help them.

When a marriage was arranged by a girl's parents, with or without her consent, it was apt to be with a man in mature life and established position. The would-be husband made large presents to the girl's parents and relatives. When the time came for the marriage, the girl was well dressed, mounted on a pony, and accompanied by four old men, she was taken to the lodge of her husband. Young men derided this kind of marriage, saying, "an old man cannot win a girl; he can win only her parents."

A man rarely had more than two wives and these were generally sisters or aunt and niece. These complex families were usually harmonious and sometimes there seemed to be little difference in the feeling of the children toward the two women who were wives to their father.

If a man abused his wife, she left him and her conduct was justified by her relations and by tribal opinion. As the tent or dwelling always belonged to the woman, the unkind husband found himself homeless. The young children generally remained with the mother, although the father's brothers would be expected to assist the woman in their support. . . . Generally speaking, the family was fairly stable; tribal sentiment did not favor the changing of the marriage relation from mere caprice.

WINNEBAGO MARRIAGE CUSTOMS

Young girls and women are also encouraged to fast to obtain the war honors.

Fasting at puberty by girls was inseparably connected with their retirement to menstrual lodges. Sometimes there was only one girl in each menstrual lodge, sometimes there were as many as three. When a woman is finished in the menstrual lodge, she bathes herself and puts on an entirely new suit of clothes. Then her home is purified with red-cedar leaves and all the sacred bundles and medicines removed. Only then can she enter her parents' lodge. As soon as she returns to her parents' lodge after her first menstrual flow she is regarded as ready to be wooed and married.

Girls were usually married as soon as they reached marriageable age, and the same was probably true of men. In most cases marriage was arranged by the parents of the young peo-

(Excerpt from Paul Radin, *The Winnebago Tribe,* Thirty-seventh Annual Report of the Bureau of American Ethnology, Smithsonian Institution, Washington, D.C., 1923)

ple, and it rarely happened that they refused to abide by the decision—a fact that seems to have been due not so much to implicit obedience as to the wise precautions taken by the parents in mating their children. . . . In former times children were betrothed to each other at an early age. At the betrothal presents were exchanged between the parents. . . .

Generally a man took but one wife, although he was permitted to marry more than one if he wished. In polygamous marriages the second wife was usually a niece or a sister of the first wife. It was the wife who often induced her husband to marry her own niece. This she did if she noticed that he was getting tired of her or losing his interest in her.

There was no ceremony connected with marriage. As soon as the customary presents were exchanged, the man came to the woman's lodge and the marriage was consummated.

A man generally lived with his parents-in-law during the first two years after his marriage. During these two years he was practically the servant of his father-in-law, hunting, fishing, and performing minor services for him. After the first two years he returned to his father's lodge, where his seat had always been kept for him. With his own folks he stayed as long as he wished, leaving it generally as soon as he had one child. . . .

In the olden times, when it was customary for those Winnebago who lived in permanent villages to occupy the long gable-roofed lodges that frequently were large enough to house as many as 40 people, the man and his family generally alternated between parents.

SIOUX MAIDEN'S FEAST

One bright summer morning, while we were still at our meal of jerked buffalo meat, we heard the herald of the Wahpeton band upon his calico pony as he rode around our circle.

(Excerpt from Charles Alexander Eastman, *Indian Boyhood,* McClure, Phillips & Co., New York, 1902)

"White Eagle's daughter, the maiden Red Star, invites all the maidens . . . to come and partake of her feast. It will be in the Wahpeton camp, before the sun reaches the middle of the sky. All pure maidens are invited. Red Star also invites the young men to be present, to see that no unworthy maiden should join in the feast."

The herald soon completed the rounds of the different camps, and it was not long before the girls began to gather in great numbers.

This particular feast was looked upon as a semi-sacred affair. It would be desecration for any to attend who was not perfectly virtuous. Hence it was regarded as an opportune time for the young men to satisfy themselves as to who were the virtuous maids of the tribe.

There were apt to be surprises before the end of the day. Any young man was permitted to challenge any maiden whom he knew to be unworthy. But woe to him who could not prove his case. It meant little short of death to the man who endeavored to disgrace a woman without cause.

The youths had a similar feast of their own, in which the eligibles were those who had never spoken to a girl in the way of courtship. It was considered ridiculous so to do before attaining some honor as a warrior, and the novices prided themselves greatly upon their self-control.

From the various camps the girls came singly or in groups, dressed in bright-colored calicoes or in heavily fringed and beaded buck-skin. Their smooth cheeks and the central part of their glossy hair was touched with vermillion. All brought with them wooden basins to eat from. . . .

The maidens' circle was formed about a cone-shaped rock which stood upon its base. This was painted red. Beside it two new arrows were lightly stuck into the ground. This is a sort of altar, to which each maiden comes before taking her assigned place in the circle, and lightly touches first the stone and then the arrows. By this oath she declares her purity. Whenever a girl approaches the altar there is a stir among the spectators, and sometimes a rude youth would call out:

"Take care! You will overturn the rock, or pull out the arrows!"

Such a remark makes the girls nervous, and especially one who is not sure of her composure.

Immediately behind the maidens' circle is the old women's or chaperons' circle. This second circle is almost as interesting to look at as the inner one. The old women watched every movement of their respective charges with the utmost concern, having previously instructed them how they should conduct themselves in any event.

The whole population of the region had assembled, and the maidens came shyly into the circle. The simple ceremonies observed prior to the serving of the food were in progress, when among a group of Wahpeton Sioux young men there was a stir of excitement. All the maidens glanced nervously toward the scene of the disturbance. Soon a tall youth emerged from the throng of spectators and advanced toward the circle. Every one of the chaperons glared at him as if to deter him from his purpose. But with a steady step he passed them by and approached the maidens' circle.

At last he stopped behind a pretty Assiniboine maiden of good family and said:

"I am sorry, but, according to custom, you should not be here."

The girl arose in confusion, but she soon recovered her self-control.

"What do you mean?" she demanded, indignantly. "Three times you have come to court me, but each time I have refused to listen to you. I turned my back upon you. Twice I was with Mashtinna. She can tell the people that this is true. The third time I had gone for water when you intercepted me and begged me to stop and listen. I refused because I did not know you. My chaperon, Makatopawee, knows that I was gone but a few minutes. I never saw you anywhere else."

The young man was unable to answer this unmistakable statement of facts, and it became apparent that he had sought to revenge himself for her repulse.

"Woo! woo! Carry him out!" was the order of the chief of the Indian police, and the audacious youth was hurried away into the nearest ravine to be chastised.

The young woman who had thus established her good name returned to the circle, and the feast was served. The "maidens' song" was sung, and four times they danced in a ring around the altar. Each maid as she departed once more took her oath to remain pure until she should meet her husband.

HIDATSA COURTING CUSTOMS

The youths of the village used to go about all the time seeking the girls; this indeed was almost all they did. Of course, when the girls were on the [garden] watcher's stage the boys were pretty sure to come around. Sometimes two youths came together, sometimes but one. If there were relatives at the watcher's stage the boys would stop and drink or eat; they did not try to talk to the girls, but would come around smiling and try to get the girls to smile back.

A girl that was not a youth's sweetheart, never talked to him. This rule was observed at all times. Even when a boy was a girl's sweetheart, or "love-boy," as we called him, if there were other persons around, she did not talk to him, unless these happened to be relatives.

Boys who came out to the watchers' stage, getting no encouragement from the girls there, soon went away.

A very young girl was not permitted to go to the watcher's stage unless an old woman went along to take care of her. In olden days, mothers watched their daughters very carefully.

Most of the songs that were sung on the watchers' stage were love songs, but not all.

One that little girls were fond of singing—girls that is of about twelve years of age—was as follows:

(Excerpt by Buffalo-bird Woman from Gilbert L. Wilson, *Agriculture of the Hidatsa Indians: An Indian Interpretation,* Univ. of Minnesota studies in the Social Sciences, No. 9, 1977).

You bad boys, you are all alike!
Your bow is like a bent basket hoop;
You poor boys, you have to run on the prairie barefoot;
Your arrows are fit for nothing but to shoot up into the sky!

Here is another song, sung by a girl to another whom she
loves as her own sister. We call her "ikupa," which has about
the same meaning as your word chum.

"My ikupa, what do you wish to see?" you said to me.
What I wish to see is the corn silk coming out on the growing
    ears;
But what *you* wish to see is that naughty young man coming!

Here is a song that we sang to tease young men that were
going by:

You young men of the Dog society, you said to me,
"When I go to the east on a war party, you will hear news of
    me, how brave I am!"
I have heard news of you;
When the fight was on, you ran and hid! And you think you
    are a brave young man! Behold, you have joined the Dog
    society. Therefore, I call you just plain dog!

COURTING AT THE CORN HARVEST

Having arrived at the field, and started a fire for the feast,
all of our family who had come out to work sat down and
began to husk the corn. Word had been sent beforehand that
we were going to give a husking feast, and the invited helpers
soon appeared. There was no particular time set for their coming, but we expected them in one of the morning hours.

(Excerpt from Gilbert L. Wilson, told by Buffalo-bird Woman)

For the most part these were young men from nineteen to thirty years of age, but a few old men would probably be in the company; and these were welcomed and given a share of the feast.

There might be twenty-five or thirty of the young men. They were paid for their labor with the most given them to eat; and each carried a sharp stick on which he skewered the meat he could not eat, to take home.

The husking season was looked upon as a time of jollity; and youths and maidens dressed and decked themselves for the occasion.

Of course each young man gave particular help to the garden of his sweetheart. Some girls were more popular than others. The young men were apt to vie with one another at the husking pile of an attractive girl.

Some of the young men rode ponies, and when her corn pile had been husked, a youth would sometimes lend his pony to his sweetheart for her to carry home her corn. She loaded the pony with loose ears in bags, bound on either side of the saddle, or with strings of braided corn laid upon the pony's back.

COURTING IN SIOUX TIPI CAMPS

Indian courtship is very peculiar in many respects; but when you study their daily life you will see the philosophy of their etiquette of love-making. There was no parlor courtship; the life was largely out-of-doors, which was very favorable to the young men.

In a nomadic life where the female members of the family have entire control of domestic affairs, the work is divided among them all. Very often the bringing of the wood and water devolves upon the young maids, and the spring or the woods

(Excerpt from Charles Alexander Eastman, *Indian Boyhood,* McClure, Phillips & Co., New York, 1902)

become the battle-ground of love's warfare. The nearest water may be some distance from the camp, which is all the better. Sometimes, too, there is no wood to be had; and in that case, one would see the young women scattered all over the prairie, gathering buffalo chips for fuel.

This is the way the red men go about to induce the aboriginal maids to listen to their suit. As soon as the youth has returned from the war-path or the chase, he puts on his porcupine-quill embroidered moccasins and leggings, and folds his best robe about him. He brushes his long, glossy hair with a brush made from the tail of the porcupine, perfumes it with scented grass or leaves, then arranges it in two plaits with an otter skin or some other ornament. If he is a warrior, he adds an eagle feather or two.

If he chooses to ride, he takes his best pony. He jumps upon its bare back, simply throwing a part of his robe under him to serve as a saddle, and holding the end of a lariat tied about the animal's neck. He guides him altogether by the motions of his body. These wily ponies seem to enter into the spirit of the occasion, and very often capture the eyes of the maid by their graceful movements, in perfect obedience to their master.

The general custom is for the young men to pull their robes over their heads, leaving only a slit to look through. Sometimes the same is done by the maiden—especially in public courtship.

He approaches the girl while she is coming from the spring. He takes up his position directly in her path. If she is in a hurry or does not care to stop, she goes around him; but if she is willing to stop and listen she puts down on the ground the vessel of water she is carrying.

Very often at the first meeting the maiden does not know who her lover is. He does not introduce himself immediately, but waits until a second meeting. Sometimes she does not see his face at all; and then she will try to find out who he is and what he looks like before they meet again. If he is not a desirable suitor, she will go with her chaperon and end the affair there.

There are times when maidens go in twos, and then there must be two young men to meet them.

There is some courtship in the night time; either in the early part of the evening, on the outskirts of dances and other public affairs, or after everybody is supposed to be asleep. This is the secret courtship. The youth may pull up the tentpins just back of his sweetheart and speak with her during the night. He must be a smart young man to do that undetected, for the grandmother, her chaperon, is usually "all ears."

Elopements are common. There are many reasons for a girl or a youth to defer their wedding. It may be from personal pride of one or both. The well-born are married publicly, and many things are given away in their honor. The maiden may desire to attend a certain number of maidens' feasts before marrying. The youth may be poor, or he may wish to achieve another honor before surrendering to a woman.

Sometimes a youth is so infatuated with a maiden that he will follow her to any part of the country, even after their respective bands have separated for the season. I know of one such case. Patah Tankah had courted a distant relative of my uncle for a long time. There seemed to be some objection to him on the part of the girl's parents, although the girl herself was willing.

The large camp had been broken up for the fall hunt, and my uncle's band went one way, the young man's family went in the other direction. After three days' travelling, we came to a good hunting-ground, and made camp. One evening somebody saw the young man. He had been following his sweetheart and sleeping out-of-doors all that time, although the nights were already frosty and cold. He met her every day in secret and she brought him food, but he would not come near the teepee. Finally her people yielded, and she went back with him to his band.

When we lived our natural life, there was much singing of

war songs, medicine, hunting and love songs. Sometimes there were few words or none, but everything was understood by the inflection. From this I have often thought that there must be a language of dumb beasts.

The crude musical instrument of the Sioux, the flute, was made to appeal to the susceptible ears of the maidens late into the night. There comes to me now the picture of two young men with their robes over their heads, and only a portion of the hand-made and carved "chotanka," the flute, protruding from its folds. I can see all the maidens slyly turning their heads to listen. Now I hear one of the youths begin to sing a plaintive serenade as in days gone by:

> "Listen! You will hear of him—
>   Hear of him who loves you!
> Maiden, you will hear of him—
>   Hear of him who loves you, who loves you!
> Listen! he will shortly go
> Seeking your ancestral foe!

Wasula feels that she must come out, but she has no good excuse, so she stirs up the embers of the fire and causes an unnecessary smoke in the teepee. Then she has an excuse to come out and fix up the tent flaps. She takes a long time to adjust these pointed ears of the teepee, with their long poles, for the wind seems to be unsettled.

Finally "chotanka" ceases to be heard. In a moment a young man appears ghost-like at the maiden's side.

"So it is you, is it?" she asks.

"Is your grandmother in?" he inquires.

"What a brave man you are, to fear an old woman! We are free; the country is wide. We can go away, and come back when the storm is over."

"Ho," he replies. "It is not that I fear her, or the consequences of an elopement. I fear nothing except that we may be separated!"

The girl goes into the lodge for a moment, then slips out once more. "Now," she exclaims, "to the wood or the prairie! I am yours!" They disappear into the darkness.

BLACKFOOT TIPI-CREEPING ON THE CANADIAN PRAIRIES

When I was young, parents were still very strict with their children—especially the girls. When boys start to have girlfriends, they have to figure out all kinds of ways to sneak around and meet with each other. The ones who were pretty brave used to go right into the tipis where their girls lived, way late, after everybody was asleep. Sometimes some pretty funny things happened that way.

One time I was going around with my best friend, singing around the Sun Dance camp late at night, as was our custom. We stopped by this white tent that belonged to a Blood family. Inside there was a real pretty girl—we were all after her, she was so nice. My friend and I crawled under a wagon, by this tent, to take a rest. Pretty soon two other fellows came along— they were older than us. They didn't see us resting in the dark. The one fellow told the other, "I'll go in first, and you watch for me. Scratch on the tent if anybody comes along."

This was a new white tent that the girl was living in. It had a picket rope that went down the front. They pulled the picket pin up so the rope would be out of the way. But the one who was staying out tied the end of that rope to his friend's overalls. The one going in didn't know it. He went on in and there was a tin stove in the way. It was dark, and he must have tripped over something. Pretty soon we heard the stove rattle and a dog jumped up and started barking. The fellow just threw himself out the door and started running. Then the rope gave out and it looked just like somebody threw him back into the tent. He

---

(Told by Ben Calf Robe at our kitchen table in 1977)

jumped back up and started running again, and the same thing happened. By this time the dog was really barking and everybody in the tent was awake. My friend and I were laughing like crazy. Finally he noticed that the rope was tied to his overalls and he tore it off and ran away. All the dogs were barking in the camp, and the neighbors were calling out to see what was going on.

Another time two friends went to a tipi where their girlfriend lived. One stayed outside and watched while the other one snuck in. He knew where the girl was sleeping, but he didn't know that she had a small hawk for a pet. Sometimes, in the past, the people used to keep wild birds and animals for pets. The hawk was perched on one of the backrests by the girl's bed. When the boy got close, the bird made a sound, like "Hagh, hagh." The boy thought it was his sweetheart calling to him, and he went closer. "Hagh, hagh," the bird said. The boy whispered, "What are you saying?" The bird just kept going, "Hagh, hagh." Finally the boy put his hand on the backrest to lean down, and the bird scratched him and bit him on the hand. The boy jumped up and got scared, and the bird screamed loud and flapped his wings, and everybody in the tipi woke up. The boy ran out real quick!"

CHAPTER SIX

Some Childhood Stories

A TYPICAL SUMMER DAY
FOR A HIDATSA BOY

I will now describe a typical day's herding by boys. Let us suppose that I was about fourteen or fifteen years of age, and that the time of year was about the present date. I recollect very well what occurred one particular day about this time of the year and will tell about it.

I arose after the sun was up, probably about eight or nine o'clock. Often, though not always, I went for a morning bath in the Missouri. In that case I proceeded to the river in moccasins, breechclout, and robe. While I bathed, I drank great quantities of the river water. When I was through bathing, I drew on my robe.... Sometimes ... I rubbed my body with white clay. This made my body feel light. I let my hair hang loose, as it was wet from the bath in the river.

I returned home and put on my leggings and my shirt of white sheeting. Although I did not always wear my leggings during the night, I had slept in both leggings and shirt the previous night, but had taken them off to go to the bath. If I slept

(Told by Wolf Chief, August 1913, excerpt from Gilbert L. Wilson, *"The Horse and the Dog in Hidatsa Culture,"* American Museum Press, New York, 1924).

without my leggings, I always laid them beside my bed in readiness for the morning.

The rest of the family had eaten their morning meal while I was at the river. My mother gave me my breakfast when I came in. In a wooden bowl she had put boiled dried meat and a mess of parched cornmeal boiled with dried squash. She had parched the corn in a frying pan until brown, stirring it with a stick to keep from burning. She pounded the parched grain to meal in a wooden mortar. When she had brought the squash to a boil, she added the meal. To eat the mess, I probably had a buffalo horn spoon. Sometimes I ate with a mussel shell, or even with one of the big spoons made of a Rocky Mountain sheep horn. The broth in which the dried meat had been boiled was served in a tin cup for a hot drink, as we now serve coffee.

Breakfast eaten, my father said to me: "It is time for you to take out the horses. Keep careful watch in the hills. If you see any strangers who look like enemies, hasten back to the village. Leave your lariat on the neck of your saddle horse and let it drag, so that if an enemy appears, you can quickly catch your horse."

My mother handed me my midday lunch, a double handful of whole parched corn, mixed with minced pieces of dried kidney fats. It was tied up in a heart skin which I fastened by a string to my belt over my left hip. I also picked out four long ears of white corn from the harvest of the previous year and tied them up, in a piece of cloth. Around this bundle I passed a piece of thong, tied the ends in a loop, passed my left arm through the loop, and so carried the bundle slung on my left elbow.

I caught one of the mares in the corral, and put on her a halter made of a flat rawhide lariat. "That is right," said my father, "drive the horses to the river and let them swim to cool off their bodies, that they may better enjoy their grazing."

As I started off on my mare my father said, "If you meet enemies while you are guarding your horses, try to escape and return home. If you cannot escape, stand against them like a man and make good your arrows!"

I had an unbacked, self bow of chokecherry wood, and a quiver of arrows which I carried on my back. The bow case and quiver were of one piece. Of the three kinds of arrows in my quiver, five or six had iron heads and were feathered with prairie-chicken feathers; two were blunt-headed; and seven or eight were pointed wooden shafts. The last two kinds were feathered with duck or owl feathers.

The blunt-headed arrows were for birds; those with iron heads for enemies; and those of pointed wood for gophers and small game. With these last we also played arrow games. . . .

My father was an arrow maker, and had made all my arrows for me. They were therefore quite handsome. They were feathered with plumes from the wing of an owl, a prairie-chicken, or a duck. . . .

I wore my hair loose. I did not wear a braided scalplock. When an enemy fell, the first man to strike coup on his body cut out the crown; and the others who also struck coup would in a twinkling strip the whole skull of the scalp. We banged the front of our hair and combed it back. The hair was cut short below each ear. That on the back of the head was let grow, and sometimes tied in a bunch, or knot, much as white women do. In olden times, Hidsatsa women did not braid their hair as they do now, but made a knot of it over the forehead.

Well, as I have said, I drove the herd down to the river, at a place west of the village. After the horses had drunk their fill, I forced them into the water and made them swim or wade to their full depth. Then I dismounted, let my mare drink, and drove her into the water; and holding her by the lariat, I made her wade almost beyond her depth.

After watering the horses at the river, I drove them about a mile from the village, where I found some of my boy friends, who had reached the grazing grounds before me. They were Iduhic, or Stands-up, seventeen years old, and Idocic, or Garter-snake, sixteen years old. As nearly as I can recollect, I was nearly or quite fifteen years old at the time. My two friends were hunting buffalo birds, or cow birds, among the horses. These birds are dark brown or black.

After driving my horses into the grazing herd, I dismounted and hobbled my mare, leaving the long lariat on her neck with the end trailing on the ground. I found the two boys had already killed three birds, which they had laid beside their two little bundles of parched corn brought for their lunch. "Have you shot some birds already?" I asked. "Yes," they answered, "but they are getting scarce now, for we have frightened them. We find it hard to get near any now."

As I talked to the boys, I looked about me. In all directions, within a radius of a quarter or half mile, were scattered herds of horses, grazing. Boys were herding most of them, but in the distance I saw one man guarding a herd. I added my horses to those of my two friends. One of these had five horses, the other, about ten; so we had about twenty-seven in the herd we were guarding.

We now started to hunt gophers. With some hair that I pulled from the mane of my mare, I made a snare and tied it to the end of my lariat. I set the noose in a gopher's hole. Soon the gopher thrust out his head and I drew the noose taut. The little animal tried to get back into his hole, but I hurried up to it, holding on to the lariat and passing it through my hands, hand over hand. When I reached the hole I drew the gopher out and with a quick swing of the noose, dashed it against the ground, killing it. This had to be done quickly, for a gopher can bite. In this manner we caught about eight gophers, which we took to the place where we had left our lunch.

"It is now noon," said Stands-up. "I will go to the village and bring some fire." He ran off afoot. Meanwhile we other two boys went down into the timber, a quarter of a mile away, and brought some dry wood for fuel.

We were first to return, but Stands-up soon joined us bringing some coals of fire in a pail. We built a fire by placing the coals on the ground and laying little sticks on them, blow-

ing the coals with our mouths. We added larger sticks and soon
had a good fire. First we roasted the birds. A sharpened stick
was thrust into the flesh at the vent and I held the bird over the
fire with this stick, until it was roasted. The entrails were not
drawn, neither were the feathers plucked.

When roasted, I broke the bird open and threw the entrails
away. I plucked out the wing feathers and stumps of the
smaller feathers with my fingers and threw them away also. I
ate the bird, biting the flesh off with my teeth; I did not pull it
off with my fingers. We ate none of the corn with the roasted
birds at this time. Of course, each of the other boys as well as
myself roasted and ate a bird.

Then we roasted gophers. First we opened the gophers and
drew out the entrails with our fingers. The lips of the opening
made in the carcass of the gopher for the purpose of removing
the entrails were now skewered together by a spit thrust in near
the tail. The carcass was held in the fire until the hair was
singed, when it was taken out and scraped with a stick to re-
move the charred hair. It was then held about five inches from
the fire, being turned now with one side, now with the other,
toward the fire. The spit was held in the hand.

Each boy roasted the gopher he ate. In all we ate five gophers, dividing them between us equally. We left three gophers
unroasted, but before the fire died down, we singed the hair of
these three and put the carcasses away with the corn we had
brought for lunch, covering both gophers and corn with a
blanket.

We buried the fire, digging a shallow hole and raking the
coals into it. We covered the coals with dried horse dung, and
put earth over this. We knew the fire would smolder beneath
until we wanted it again.

We noticed now that some of the herders were driving their
horses to water, so we knew it was time for us to do likewise. I
caught and unhobbled my grey mare; for when I began to
snare gophers, I had taken the lariat off her neck.

There was a pond not far away, but the water was not good

to drink, as there were little worms in it. We watered our horses at the Missouri, and we ourselves drank freely and also bathed. Meanwhile we had tied our riding horses each to a good big stone, usually about a foot thick, giving the lariat a turn or two about it.

After our bath, we got our riding horses and went up the bank to find the rest of the herd already half way back to the grazing grounds. They were going along at a leisurely pace, stopping now and then to graze. We caught up to them and drove them to our camp again. Here I hobbled my mare, letting the lariat drag.

We now ate our parched corn. We opened the fire, and found the coals still glowing. We added fuel and roasted the three gophers we had saved, each boy eating one. The gophers were fat and made us feel good. I also parched two of the ears of corn I had brought. I made a little bed of coals, laid the ears of corn upon it, and rolled them about with a stick, until they were parched brown. I liked corn parched in this way. The two ears I had not used, I kept to take back home with me. "These are fine ears," I thought. "I chose them because they were the most select and I may want them again."

"After our meal we began again to catch gophers; but as we had been hunting them all morning, they had become frightened and were slow to show themselves. "I know how to catch these gophers," said Garter-snake at last. "Once before when I was hunting them, they became frightened and did not show themselves, and we poured water down their holes. This made them come up."

"You go to the village and bring us a pail," said Stands-up and Garter-snake to me. I ran off to the village and soon returned with the pail. We also had the small one in which we had brought the fire. We filled the two pails at the pond and brought them to a gopher hole. We dug out the top of the hole with a knife to a depth of about seven inches and a diameter of five inches. This was to make a kind of funnel into which to pour the water. Garter-snake emptied one pail, I the second.

We each stood ready with a stick. We found two gophers in this hole and killed them both. As they were dripping wet, we laid them in the sun near our fireplace to dry.

"Let us now shoot at a mark," said Stands-up. He took one of his wooden pointed arrows, thrust it by the feathered end into the ground, and upon the point stuck a small ball of horse dung. We went about thirty yards away. "Let us shoot two arrows each," said Stands-up. "Whoever hits the ball of dung shall have the two gophers we drowned out of the hole."

"You shoot first," said Garter-snake to me. I shot my arrows quite close to the mark. Garter-snake and Stands-up shot, neither hitting the mark. The second round, Garter-snake shot first, Stands-up shot second, and I third. We used only sharp wooden arrows. As soon as one shot, he ran and picked up his arrow.

The third round, Garter-snake shot first, hitting the ball of dung the first time. "There," he cried, "I eat the two gophers." He disembowled them and made ready to roast them. "Now," he said, "I will give you two boys one of the gophers to divide between you. But while I am roasting them, see if you cannot catch another, and I will have my share of it."

"Agreed," I cried. Stands-up and I filled the two pails at the pond, and listening a few moments, heard w-s-s-s-s! the hissing bark of a gopher. We looked and spied the gopher; he dived into his hole.

"It may not be a deep hole," said Stands-up, as he emptied the smaller of the pails which he held. The gopher did not come up. Stands-up filled the hole with water from the larger pail and as the gopher dashed out, he killed it with a blow of his bow. Drowned from their holes, gophers were easy to kill as they came up with their eyes shut, no doubt on account of the water.

I took the dead gopher to Garter-snake. "Here is the gopher you wanted," I said. "Good," he answered. "Now you roast it." I did so, and he said, "We agreed to divide this gopher, but I think it would be better if we shot again for it."

"Agreed," said Garter-snake. "Whoever shoots the farthest, shall eat this gopher." "Then I shall eat it," laughed Stands-up, as he shot. I followed, but my arrow failed to fly as far as his.

Garter-snake took up his bow. "I am sorry," he said, "that your arrows did not go farther. Now watch me!" He had a sinew backed bow. He put an arrow on the string, drew it, and though he aimed at a rather low angle, his arrow went farthest of the three. We had shot with wooden pointed arrows.

"Now," said Garter-snake, "this is my gopher; but I am going to divide it with you, only I will take the chest, the best part. You boys may eat the back part. I don't like it anyway." We divided the gopher, Garter-snake eating the fore quarters, and Stands-up and myself the hind quarters.

It was now about three o'clock in the afternoon.

Other boys who had been herding their horses some distance away now came up, and we had a sham battle on horseback. We used roundheaded, or blunt, arrows. In the group were about ten boys, all of about the same age as my companions and I. Butterfly and Fingernail, I remember, were two of the boys.

We practiced fancy riding. One boy would ride along, dismount, and mount again, at a gallop. Another boy stood with his bow ready; a second boy galloped up near him, dropped on the farther side of his horse and swerved past, while the boy with the bow shot at the rider's horse.

Sometimes I galloped up to a boy, hidden behind my horse with only my leg exposed over the pony's back. The boy could see nothing but this exposed leg as I approached him. I struck him as I would an enemy; but as I galloped away, he shot at me as he was now able to see my body. Of course, as I galloped away, my horse turned, exposing my body to the other boy's arrow.

The easiest way to mount a horse [with no saddle] is to put the left elbow forward over the back of the horse, seize the horse's mane with the right hand and leap up, lying on the abdomen transversely over the horse's back; then throw the left leg over and rise to a sitting position. In battle we could not be so deliberate as we ran the risk of being shot at by the enemy. We boys therefore practiced leaping from our ponies and mounting them again at a gallop. Seizing the mane with the right hand, one leaped from the right front, with the left foot lifted high, and vaulted on the horse's back at one bound.

Then we played that I was thrown from my horse, or that my horse had been killed; and another boy rode forward to save me, carrying me off on his pony with him. The rescuer stopped his pony; I ran forward, placed both hands on the horse's hips and leaped up behind the other, very much as white children play leap-frog. Being trained to this, the horse did not kick. . . . All these games were intended as preparation for battle, for all the boys expected to go to war as they grew older. In these pony games I always rode my old gray mare.

We next practiced archery for a long while, using our bows again as we thought we would do in battle. We put a stick in the ground and shot at it, just to see who was the best shot; or, we took turns, each boy running forward, stopping suddenly, and shooting instantly. Very often a boy dashed past the mark, shooting at it as he ran. Sometimes the boys shot at one another, being careful, however, not to shoot hard. The boy who was the target tried to dodge the arrow, springing to right or left, or dropping suddenly so that the arrow passed by or over him. Only blunt arrows were used, at a distance of twenty or thirty yards. We practiced dodging arrows, because we expected to have to do so in war.

Of course we guarded our horses all the time of our play, keeping our saddle horses close by and in readiness for any emergency. No matter what our play, we watched our herd and had our saddle horses ready.

We now mounted our horses, drove the whole herd to the river and watered them. I cut out my bunch of horses from the herd, the other boys cut out theirs, and we all returned to the village, arriving a little before sundown.

I drove my horses to my father's door, dismounted, and

went in. My father was lying on his bed. "Are all the horses here?" he asked. "They are outside," I answered. "Good, I will attend to them," he said.

The other members of the family had already eaten their evening meal. I spread my blanket on the earth floor between the two forward main posts of the lodge and my mother brought me my supper in a wooden feast bowl, with a big Rocky Mountain sheep horn spoon to eat with. The mess was hominy of pounded yellow corn, boiled with beans, and seasoned with spring salt-alkali salt, gathered from the edge of a spring. It was a dish that I liked.

CHILDHOOD MEMORIES OF WILLIE EAGLE PLUME

I am Atsitsina (Prairie-Owl Man), a Blood Indian, born in "the year the mountain fell" [Frank Slide, 1903, when part of a mountain came down, known as Frank Slide, burying the town of Frank, Alberta, not far from the Blood Indian Reserve]. I was born in the old Indian way, although I have learned a lot of the white man's way since then.

My father was called Eagle Plume, because he once stole a prized racehorse from an enemy camp, and this horse had an eagle plume tied in its hair. My father took more than ten scalps from enemies on his war trails. He was one of the leading warriors in our tribe, and I grew up feeling proud to be his son.

When I was born, my father was also known as Natosina, or Sun Chief. It was a name he inherited from a great medicine man of his own young days. By this time my father was a medicine man, too. The war and buffalo days had ended about twenty years before. We were at peace, and my father spent a lot of his time praying for people, doctoring them, and leading

(Told at our kitchen table in 1975)

religious ceremonies for the tribe. My mother helped him with his work, and so did his other two wives; all three were related.

Because my father had several wives, I now have a brother who is only six months older. His name is Fred Eagle Plume, though in Blackfoot we know him by the name Earth. His mother was my dad's first wife. She married him while still a young and pure girl, so she was allowed to put up the Medicine Lodge, or Sun Dance ceremony. My mother, Sikskiaki (Black-Faced Woman) could not do this with him because she had been married earlier. Her first husband, Low Horn, was killed when his wagon overturned and trapped him in a puddle of water. My mother, and her children from him, were able to escape. They had been on the way to a Sun Dance.

As I said, I was proud to be Eagle Plume's son—other people treated me with respect on account of my father, and their kids envied me. But my father did not spend much time with me. His work was very serious, and there were a lot of rules and regulations he had to follow. Kids are good at breaking rules, so we were not much allowed around him when he was busy. Instead, his mother—my grandmother, Otsani—took care of me a lot of the time. She was my real hero.

My grandmother still used a travois on her horse, when she traveled around. By this time most of the people in our tribe had wagons; some even owned those fancy buggies with fringe on top. But she liked her old horse and travois. I rode them both, and I liked them, too.

Grandma's horse was an old gray mare, and she used it mostly to go down in the river bottom for firewood and water. She used to bundle me up in a blanket and tie me on top of the little frame she built with thin poles over her travois. I was quite small at this time, but I still recall the strange, bumpy rides, looking backward, while my grandmother was leading the horse ahead. Sometimes my brothers and cousins were tied on with me, and we would make too much noise for the old lady, so she'd tell us to shut up.

But I was Otsani's pet, and she never got angry at me, even

if I was with the crowd that woke her up when she was nap-
ping, or played tricks on her, like tying the laces of her moccasins together while she was asleep, or nailing her front door
shut from outside! Sometimes we tied the legs of her old horse
together, and she'd have a hard time figuring out why it
wouldn't go. She was in her eighties and couldn't see too well
anymore.

Sometimes a bunch of us kids would go down into the
bushes with Otsani to help her gather wood and pick berries.
After the work we would go swimming, while the old lady took
a rest. She used to call me to her while the others were still
playing, and she would unbraid and comb my hair. All the
boys of that time wore their hair long—just like our fathers.
She used a brush made from a porcupine's tail, dried, with a
stick inserted for a handle. She made me feel very special at
those times—I still get a very good feeling by thinking about
them.

I wore a breechcloth all the time when I was small. I didn't
know anything about store-bought underwear. My grandmother made breechcloths for me from soft buckskin she had
tanned herself. She also made moccasins for me from the same
thing. The leggings that I remember best were made from a
white woolen blanket with colored stripes. She made them so
that the stripes matched on both leggings and ran crosswise
down my lower legs. Compared with the jeans and shirts I
wear now, these old-time Indian clothes sound uncomfortable.
The leggings were always coming untied from my belt and
slipping down on one side or the other. The breechcloth could
be even more awkward. But I don't remember getting cold on
the exposed parts of my body, nor worrying about being awkward. It was all I had then, and I enjoyed my childhood.

My favorite shirt at that time was one my grandmother cut
and sewed for me, by hand, out of a large flour sack. It was soft
and warm, but the best part was the horned head of an elk
printed in color on both sides, along with a bunch of fancy
writing. The shirt was made so that the elk heads were on my

chest and back, and I sure was proud of them. I guess it was an early version of those decorated shirts young people wear nowadays!

My coat was made from a blanket, in the style of capotes first seen on French trappers, who came into our country in the early 1800s. It had no pockets, but a long, pointed hood hung down behind. In this hood I used to stash my goodies, including the treats my grandmother gave me to eat while I was out playing—mostly bits of dried meat and berries, sometimes candy from the trading posts.

My father always had lots of horses, so I've been riding all my life. Otsani started to put me on the back of her old gray mare when I was three or four. That horse was so gentle, kids could play around its legs and not bother it at all. Young kids were often tied to saddles on the backs of tame horses like this, and left for hours at a time, while the animal grazed at the end of a rope. I've seen kids fall asleep right in the saddle while "riding" like this.

Among my favorite childhood toys were bows and arrows. I had several sets of them, since they were forever getting lost and broken. Mostly my father made these for me, or else they were presents from various uncles. Since we boys had no money for betting with in our various games and races, we often used arrows and sometimes bows. My father made the last bow I ever had, and this one stayed with me until after I was married. It was a real work of art, with sinew backing and a snakeskin covering, and it sure was powerful. I sometimes earned a little money in my teenage years by giving demonstrations with this bow and arrows at rodeos and fairs.

We learned to shoot our bows and arrows by hunting gophers and small birds, less often by shooting at "marks," such as tree stumps. The arrows for such shooting did not have tips, and sometimes they even lacked feathers. A father who was really fond of his little son might make him feathered arrows to use for practice, but these were eagerly sought by the older boys in betting contests! The fanciest arrows a boy of my time could own were feathered ones that were decorated right up the shaft by spiral lines. To make these, a man would peel each arrow in a long spiral, leaving behind half the bark. Then he would grease the shafts and hold them over a smoky fire until they turned dark brown. Then he would peel off the remaining bark, revealing a light spiral.

A lot of the games we played as boys would have made us tough for battle, except that the warpath days were over. Often we divided into two groups and attacked each other with dried manure, sometimes kicking or wrestling each other to the ground in the process. We did a lot of wrestling, including what is often called "Indian wrestling," where two lie on their bellies, face each other, lock hands, and try to push each other's arms down.

We didn't know much about boxing, except as a white man's "sport." Our fighting was not meant for sport, but to prepare us for battle. We kicked each other to see who was toughest, and we even shot at each other with blunt-tipped arrows. The only thing the older people told us was to treat each other with respect, even when fighting. Bullies, and ruffians who actually caused trouble were unpopular among us.

A popular game for boys of my time involved the throwing of knives, or sometimes awls. Two of us would take turns throwing a knife into the ground so it would stick, each throw being a little harder. We'd start out by throwing the knife with each pair of our fingers, until we'd gone through both hands. After that we'd stand the tip of the knife on the ends of our fingers, one at a time, making it stick into the ground. Whenever the knife didn't stick, the other fellow won. In real exciting games we'd get so far that we'd stand the knife up on our heads and make it spin down before it stuck in the ground. Sometimes a boy would end up sticking himself with a knife, then he would run home crying, and the rest of us would scatter to avoid trouble.

We used to imitate the older boys, and especially the men, who told their stories of adventure around evening fires. Some of the kids had little tipis, and in them we would play "house." The boys would go out hunting for small animals, while the girls fixed up the homes and made fires. They would cook whatever we managed to shoot with our simple arrows, while we sat to one side, smoked miniature pipes, and told about our hunts. If we had no luck with hunting, we'd go on the "warpath" and raid dried meat where someone wasn't looking—often from our mothers' food bags!

Even religious ceremonies were imitated in our childhood playing. The men and women in our tribe have always had sacred societies, so we made up our own, duplicating the regalia with whatever we could find. We made sacred staffs and headdresses, decorating them with whatever feathers and bits of cloth we could find. Keep in mind that we never made fun of these things; we always had the respect taught by our parents for anything to do with prayers.

Still, I recall one thing I did as a teenage boy that must have taken me close to the border of disrespect. Since I was the daring one in our crowd, someone once said I should imitate the grown men by giving an important offering "to the Sun," during our Sun Dance celebration. Men sometimes gave weapons, prized clothing, or even bits of their own bodies, to show courage and humbleness.

This was in about my twelfth or fourteenth summer, during that time of the year when most of the tribe came together for an old-time tipi camp. The sacred lodge for the Sun had been ceremonially put up, and all that day the grown men had made offerings and told the people of their greatest adventures. In the old days this was done to make everyone in the tribe proud and courageous, especially the boys and young men.

It was the last night of the big camp, and the moon was shining brightly. I wanted to impress the other boys with my offering, but I had nothing that seemed worthy of notice. Instead, I got my brothers to help me in rolling off a fancy new buggy that was parked behind someone's unpainted tipi. We brought it to the sacred lodge, where others were watching to see what I would do. Slowly I took the buggy all apart, tying each of its pieces to the sacred lodge's special Center Pole. There I called out, like the grown-up men, but in a soft voice, "Here, Sun, I'm giving you this to show you how much I think of you," and so forth. I went on like that until I had the whole buggy hanging up.

The next morning everyone got up early to pack their camps and head back home. That's when we heard the camp announcer walking around saying, "You people, that old man White Owl has lost his carriage, please be on the lookout for it." So it wasn't long before someone brought this old man the report, "Your buggy is all in pieces, hanging up in the Sun Lodge!" My, he sure was upset, calling us "dog faces" and other mean things that were our version of swear words. He had to go and pray hard to the Sun and explain why he was taking his buggy back. Some men helped him put it back together after that. I was sure scared somebody would tell on me, and I never pulled a trick of that sort again!

Even winter was a lot of fun when I was a little kid. My father made me a real old-time sled, except that he used beef ribs instead of those from buffalo. It was just a little thing, but it sure went fast down the hills by our house. The ribs were tied together with rawhide, and a small piece of hide was stretched across to make a seat. It was my prized winter toy until some years later, when I got a big white man's sled from town.

Soon after I learned to ride by myself—when I was about six or seven—my father gave me a horse of my own! It was a little pony that grew up right around our house, just like a dog. It was so used to us children that we could wrestle with it or play around and it never caused trouble. This horse and I must have learned about riding from each other, at the same time. I used to race it and have imitation battles against my friends while pretending it was my war pony. Sometimes another boy would get on the horse with me, and we would challenge another pair, also riding a pony, to see who could drag the other off his mount.

At about that time I started going to school, down at the Stand-Off Day School, so I rode there on my pony. That was when my long hair got cut, and I began wearing store-bought clothing—"white man's dress," we called it. My father did not like the change in our appearance, but he encouraged my brother and me to learn well in school, mainly so that we'd "learn to get around among white men without being cheated," he would say.

I had a good time at this school, and I learned a bit about life during the few years I went there. I have heard about Indian children who were treated very badly in schools; even my own children were disciplined very strictly at the Catholic boarding school on our reserve. But my schooling was not so harsh, at all. Don't forget, the Bloods always defended their lands very fiercely and only settled on this reserve on their own agreement, after the buffalo died out. In my young days, our fathers were proud men who didn't let outsiders come into their home lives to push them around. This attitude has done a lot to make me satisfied in life, especially when I see how other people struggle.

At school I may have looked like any Canadian kid, at least from the back, but at home our whole family still lived pretty much like old-time Indians. We had log houses and cook stoves, but our parents spent much of their time in tipis, and we kids spent most of ours outdoors.

When I was about eleven or twelve, I started breaking horses. My older "brothers" [including cousins, and so on) dared me to do it, and I was the kind ready to take them up on it. We picked out a yearling from my dad's herd, although we didn't go to him for permission. He would have said it was too dangerous, which is probably what his dad said to him. We looked for a slim and lively horse that showed signs of becoming a good runner. One of the older fellows rode his own horse and caught this one with a rope. We led it down over the embankment, from the prairie to the river bottom, where we picked out a place with lots of deep mud. We led the horse out into the middle of this, and that's when I sloshed my way next to it and somehow pulled myself up on its back.

The poor horse was pretty tense and nervous by this time, after being roped, pulled, and surrounded by a bunch of excited boys. It tried to buck me off, getting really frantic and throwing slobber with its head, but it couldn't do much with its legs down in the mud. I finally lost my grip on the mane, while all the others yelled for me to hold on longer. But when I fell, it was only into mud, from where I jumped up and got right back on the horse again. Eventually the animal was so tired that it no longer objected to my presence, at which point the others led us out on dry land, where we all paused for a few minutes while the horse allowed me to sit still.

When my dad learned what I'd done, he didn't scold me; instead, he gave me the young horse for a present! Had I been hurt, *then* he would have scolded me!

After that I began to get a reputation for breaking horses. Eventually I quit school and began earning money by working with horses. I was still a teenager when I began competing against white cowboys in small-town rodeos. Sometimes I won a few dollars, other times I had to leave behind my winnings when bullies drove me out of town. I soon learned what my dad had meant about being cheated among the white men! Some were very good friends of mine, while others acted as if I were not much better than the horses in their corrals.

THE DEBUT OF ALOYASIUS

The roofs of the buildings at the United States Indian school were painted red. Aloyasius could not remember the time when he had not watched their glittering surfaces, looming higher still than the bare sunbaked hill which reared them

---

(A 1920s boarding-school story by Estelle Armstrong, exerpted from *The Red Man*, student newspaper of the Carlisle Indian School in Carlisle, Pennsylvania)

and which hid the muddy waters of the Colorado as it eddyed lazily along between the dirty Arizona town and the reservation of his people. At times, more often in the early morning, before the sun had dried the mists which hid the jagged mountain tops in clouds of coolness, the dazzling redness of the roofs softened and their vivid glare blended tenderly with the lights and shadows of the dreary windswept landscape. But at noonday, when Aloyasius lay half buried in the sand on the shady side of his father's mud hut, the glare of the almost tropic sun on their red expanse seemed to dissolve their color into flaming particles which scintillated dizzily in the waves of heat which rippled between him and the hill.

It was at such a time that Aloyasius hated most the sight of the Government Indian School. He had always known that sometime he must go there, tho perhaps not till the Indian Agent had discovered that he was old enough. His brothers and sisters were already there and could speak the hated English. Aloyasius could not speak English. His brothers never spoke it when they came home on Sunday for the weekly half-holiday. He knew, too, why he must go. His feeble old grandparents might not get their monthly rations unless the children were sent in; so the Indian Agent had said, and the Indian Agent was to be feared and obeyed above all else. Then, too, there was often no food in the mud hut—never was there enough—and children must be fed. At the Government School there was plenty, with meat daily and clothes to wear, and yet Aloyasius had rebelled savagely and in his childish, stolid way had resisted the fate which was forcing him under the shadow of those glaring, red roofs.

And now the day had come. His father had gruffly bidden him "catheca," and he had left the mud hut and had followed him along the narrow path which wound in and out among the rank arrow-weed, which thrust out its pale, spiny branches to entangle his bare legs, and up the steep, graveled path to the school. At the door of one of the buildings a woman was standing, and to her his father had given him. Aloyasius knew she was a woman because of her clothes, tho neither she nor they were like anything that he had ever seen, and at her hair he had marveled greatly. Perhaps it was that color because she lived under the red roofs; it was the color of them at evening, when the hot sun had set behind the western mountain peaks and the tender touch of twilight mellowed and made beautiful the things which glared by day. Aloyasius decided that it was pretty, but not pretty for hair. He liked hair that hung straight and black to one's waist, as his father's did, and tied with strings of many colors.

Strange as the woman looked, she did things still more strange. She had taken him into a room where a big tub stood in one corner and she had filled the tub with clear, cool water. To Aloyasius, water—clear water like this, not muddy as it came from the river—was something infinitely precious and not to be wasted. The women of his people carried it on their heads down the steep path from the school, in the large tin cans which the school cook gave them after they were emptied of their contents of syrup, and only at times had he been allowed to drink all he wanted. But this woman had taken off his shirt—Aloyasius nearly always wore his shirt; only when the sun was hottest did he go quite naked—and had made him understand that he was to get into the tub of water. His black eyes widened with fear and he looked at the woman doubtfully. It must be the color of her hair that made her do such strange things, he thought, but he had obediently climbed in and she had taken a cloth and something smooth and slippery that made a white foam when she rubbed it, and had washed him. She got the white foam in his eyes and mouth and they smarted, but Aloyasius was too surprised to mind. The amazed idea of being washed, *all over,* stampeded for the first time all other emotions.

She had let him wipe himself dry and had showed him how to put on the new clothes—the things which stuck so close to his skin—then a shirt and a pair of long Khaki pants, like the ones the Indian police wore. Aloyasius revered and envied the

Indian police, with their short gun at the hip and their belt with cartridges all around, and he hoped the woman had gone to get him a belt and gun also. She had only a comb in her hand when she returned and she had made him sit down while she combed the "neeill" out of his hair.

Aloyasius knew very well that there were "neeill" in his hair; there always had been and he had supposed they belonged there and had accepted them without questioning, as he had the thirst and poor food and the stones which bruised his bare feet. That these things could be remedied had never occurred to him, nor to his people, but this woman combed his head till it was clean, and stopped it with kerosene. He was troubled, tho already he knew that this woman with the strange hair, who had so suddenly shot into his little Yuma orbit, would do him no harm. Her touch was much kinder than his mother's, who left him to do much as he pleased as long as he tended the one poor pony and stoned away the dogs from the family meal as it cooked in a kettle over the open fire.

When the dinner bell sounded Aloyasius went with the other children to the dining room. Here they sat on stools at tables, and a man had tucked a white cloth under his chin. He had no idea why the cloth was put there, but as all the other boys had them on he concluded that it was still another strange article of clothing. It kept unfastening and slipping into his lap, and he wondered why it didn't go on with buttons, as all the other clothes did. Poor little Aloyasius! He had wondered over so many strange things that his brown head was fairly dizzy and his brain felt as tho it was done up in curl papers.

He tried to use his spoon and fork to eat with, as the man told him, but they got in his way and he was still hungry when the gong sounded and the children took off the pieces of white cloth and folded them beside their plates. Aloyasius did the same, wondering the while why anything should be worn for so short a time. He wore his shirt at home for weeks and weeks, without thought of any change. But they did strange things under these red roofs. The roofs had come to be typical to him of the many clothes with the many buttons which all wore who lived under them. Aloyasius soon learned that the long pants and shirt were his play clothes and when the bell rang after dinner was over—it seemed to him that the bell was always ringing for him to unbutton one set of clothes and button another—the woman had given him a pair of short black pants that stopped above his knees and fitted his round limbs so closely that they seemed to have grown on him. They were very tight, and when he bent over to lace the stiff new shoes something had happened to them behind and the women had made him take them off and had sewed the rent with strong thread, and one of the boys told him to sit down to lace his shoes and not bend over again.

Aloyasius had been eagerly curious at school, watching the many wonderful happenings with uncomprehending eyes. There was another woman here, only she had black hair more like his own, and Aloyasius decided that he liked her better than the woman with hair like the roofs, who made him change his clothes so often, and wash his face and hands many, many times a day. The why of the numberless unfamiliar occurrences was fast enveloping him in a cloud of distrust and doubt. Why must he wash and wear so many clothes and eat with pointed things instead of his fingers? Aloyasius thought if only he could know why these things had to be he would do them much more cheerfully.

When school was over he had had to change from his schoolclothes to his play clothes before he could go out to play. Then had come supper, with the white cloth that wouldn't stay on; then more play and then bed. Aloyasius was not accustomed to elaborate ceremonies attending his retirement for the night and the sight of so many narrow white beds, side by side in a big room with wide, iron-barred windows, made him open his eyes in astonishment, and the tightening in his throat caused him to catch his breath with a sob. The woman showed him where he was to lie, and helped him off with his clothes, all his clothes this time, even those that stuck so close to his skin—and gave him a long, loose thing, like a girl's dress, to put on. Aloyasius found when he had struggled into it that it had buttons on the back, and he wondered with all the powers that the long day of wonderment had left to him why going to bed under the red roofs was so very different from going to bed in his father's hut.

His brother had told him in his own tongue that he must get down and say his prayers before he got into bed and Aloyasius stood uncertain, not knowing quite how to go about it. He had oftentimes gone to the little Mission on the reservation and had learned to kneel at certain times, but to kneel at night before you went to sleep was queer. He crept between white sheets and lay very still. His heart ached for his corner in the sand at home where he curled up at night with his mother's gay shawl, or his father's coat, thrown over him. He drew the despised government blanket over his throbbing head and cried his little heart out beneath the shelter of the glaring, red roofs.

THE RETURN

The old squaws, sitting squat on the platform beside their mounds of beadwork, looked at Jose as he swung himself from the day coach of the Overland and nudged each the other in derision of his uniform and close-cut hair. Sitting there with their cheap, gaudy strings of beads held up to catch some unwary tourist's eye, their hair long and dank over shapeless, ugly shoulders, their grimy faces impassive with the peculiar expressionless stare of the hopeless, the old women seemed the very incarnation of the spirit of ridicule against which nearly every returned student is pitted on his return from school to his reservation home.

The innate hatred of the older Indians for the white man's

(By Estelle Armstrong, from *The Red Man,* student newspaper of the Carlisle Indian School in Carlisle, Pennsylvania, 1925)

dominating activity, with its resulting absorption of their own purposeless lives, eggs them on to use in retaliation the only weapon left them, often undoing by their witless ridicule of returned students what years of study and careful training has inculcated. For you may beat an Indian in a fair fight and he will respect you; you may cheat him in a horse trade, if you can, and he will be wary of you; but expose him to ridicule before his peers and he is your enemy forever; for ridicule of his person is one thing which nature has not fitted an Indian to bear.

The evil potency of this enervating criticism is recognized by every educator of our Indian youth who has watched the returned student conquer or be conquered by it. And it is because this spirit of ridicule is not an attribute of any particular tribe or locality, but is common to every clan, whether of valley or mountain or barren plain, that I select the homecoming of Jose as typical of many such that I have witnessed, and having witnessed have marveled, not at the half failure sometimes resulting, but at the optimism that dared to expect success.

Jose had been but an indifferent student at best, mastering the intricacies of the sixth grade in his nineteenth year, the fifth and last of his term at Carlisle. But balanced against his poor classroom record was his good conduct as a student, his industry in the workshop, and his ability as an officer of Company C. In fact, he was an average student among the full-bloods, who, as a rule, do not take kindly to books and abstruse problems but with their hands do well and faithfully what is given them to do.

Jose had been 14 years old when he left the hot Arizona reservation on the Colorado and the five years had wrought many changes in the dark-skinned boy who, at nineteen, walked with head and shoulders erect and saw that his shoes were duly polished and his clothes and nails immaculate. For at fourteen Jose had slouched and shoes were unknown and clothes a concession to encroaching civilization, which he had detested. Of his early home life he had but confused memories and from his parents he had received no word in all the five years. The remembrance of the squalor and meanness of his early years had faded from his mind and his thoughts of home were a misty background of idleness and freedom against which his present life loomed portentous and grim.

And now the same forceful hand which had so deliberately taken him from his home five years before was as calmly replacing him in the groove nature had fitted him to fill, after having done all in its power to make him unsuited for it. If Jose had been given to ponder on the reason of things he might have questioned the wisdom which had separated him from his natural environment to teach him customs and habits which rendered that environment detestable, only to return him to it. Happily, Jose had no such questioning—he was going home; home to his kindred and early playmates, to the misty memories of his boyhood home.

Home! He had come to it at last, with the tropical sun beating down upon him and a strange sinking in his heart at the sight of the leering squaws at the station.

He gripped his suitcase and elbowed his way through the crowded platform, thronged with travelers, Mexicans and men of his own tribe, the latter in corduroys and light shirts, their long hair bound at the neck with gay kerchiefs and decorated at waist and elbow with strips of calico of many colors. They turned to stare at him, insolently noting his smart uniform, his cropped hair, his general well-groomed appearance, breaking into loud guffaws at his expense as he passed them. Among their number were two of Jose's early playmates, with whom he had swum the eddying Colorado in former days, sounding each treacherous sandbar and skirting dangerously close to the seething whirlpools; but he passed them now with no sign of recognition, failing to understand that one of the boyish anticipations of his homecoming had vanished in that chorus of rude laughter.

As he climbed the steep hill which skirted the Colorado and hid from view the reservation of his people, Jose felt his pulses bounding rapidly. He had not expected his parents to meet him at the train. They were very old; had been old when

Jose left five years before and had many sons, of which he was the youngest. Without thought he took the old path which led to his father's hut, the dust which lay like powder on every bush and shrub stinging his eyes and throat. He found himself wondering if this father's home was like the open, grass-thatched hovels which he passed, around which naked children stopped their play to stare at him and mongrel dogs challenged him from a safe distance. His uncertain memories of home had been largely of the freedom and unrestraint of former years and they had dealt kindly with the poor hut and the depriva-tion which had also been his portion.

An old woman raised her head from the pot of soup she was tending over a small open fire and watched him as he ap-proached, and Jose recognized his mother. Old and bent with many years, her hair matted above her sunken eyes, her only garment a shred of filth that stopped above her knees, her un-human hands ending in talons, the mother sat and watched her son draw near. The accents of his native tongue came instinc-tively to Jose's lips and he spoke hesitatingly—"mother." The sunken eyes lighted as she bent near that her dim vision might view this stranger son, and voiceless the mother held him and gazed long at his altered features and alien clothes. Then, tot-tering to a prone form lying in the sand by the side of the hut, she spoke, and her words roused the wasted figure of Jose's fa-ther. With palsied hands he shaded his eyes as he looked at his son, then rising slowly and with difficulty, his raiment a loin cloth, his gray locks streaming over his shoulders, and yet with dignity withal, he extended his hand in welcome.

As in a dream Jose sat down on a nearby log and gazed about him. He saw the mean hut in its squalor and poverty; the heaps of rags in the sand on which his parents slept; the open fire over which hung the kettle of soup containing the coming meal; the sand and greasewood glaring in the July sun. He saw the Colorado with its treacherous gleaming quicksand and just beyond the vicious frontier town, flaunting its vice so shame-lessly, and then his gaze wandered back to the form of his mother as she bent again over the pot of soup.

Four years had passed and again the July sun beat down on the familiar scene as I looked from the car window as the Overland pulled in for a stop of ten minutes. We "took on water" here and as I idly watched I recognized in the stalwart figure running down the platform with a length of hose our friend Jose.

Hastily making my way outside I called to him and as soon as his work permitted, he came, doffing his cap and hesitating to give me his hand in greeting, soiled as it was from his recent labors. His overalls and working shirt were neat and whole, his hair closely cut and his face showed no signs of dissipation beneath its grime and sweat. He looked as I believe he is, an honest youth engaged in honest work, and my heart rejoiced for him.

"O, yes," he replied to my question, "of course I am married. We have a child a year old and we are getting along just fine. I work over here at the railroad every day"; and he called good-bye as our train got under way.

Consider, you who feel called upon to judge him, to measure him by your standards, of which he falls so far short; over against your pride of birth, your mother's prayers, the sense of honor inborn, your mental capacity of assimilation, I place the forms of Jose's parents; the squalor of the mud hut; the unbridled license of his early years; the frontier town with saloon doors always open; the pointing fingers of the leering squaws; and I challenge you to declare his education vain or to proclaim his life a failure.

LITTLE-JOE'S BACK HOME

All the morning noises of Taos were sounding together, telling the people that a new day was waiting for them.

Little-Joe opened one black eye. Sleepily he looked up at

(Excerpt from Ann Clark, *Little Boy with Three Names,* Bureau of Indian Affairs, Chilocco, Oklahoma, 1940)

the long, straight, white aspen poles which made a ceiling overhead. "Where am I?" he asked himself. "What is this place around me?"

His brown hand came out from underneath the bed-cover. It went feeling about on the wool-filled pad beneath him. "This is not my white bed. Where is my white bed and all the other white beds in this dormitory?"

Little-Joe rolled over on his stomach. His head came out from the covers. It turned this way and that way. "I am just like a turtle looking out from my shell," he told himself, and laughed himself awake. Both black eyes were open now. They lighted up the slender brown face of the little Indian boy.

He knew where he was, now that he was all awake. This was his mother's house. This was his bed on the floor of the family sleeping room. Beneath him was the mattress of soft wool that once had covered his father's sheep. He saw the good earth floor, hardpacked by walking feet.

Little-Joe stretched and stretched. Today summer began and he was in Taos again.

In the outer room he heard the soft footsteps of his mother as she moved about cooking breakfast for her family. He heard his older sister, Iao, playing with the baby. Iao's voice made little running sounds like water. The baby's laughter answered like the splash of a stone in the creek.

"I am the lazy one, to lie sleeping while my family move about me. I am new here. I have just come back from school."

Little-Joe sat up. He looked around for clothes to wear. Last night he had placed his school shoes side by side near the corner fireplace. He had neatly folded his blue shirt and blue overalls and placed them on a stool beside his shoes. Down there, at the school they had taught him that way. But now his clothes were gone. Deerskin moccasins stood where the school shoes had been. A calico shirt and beaded leggings were beside them. The little blue shirt and overalls and the two school shoes were gone. There was no place in all this room for school clothes to feel at home. Everything here was new and strange to the little boy who had lived at Boarding School.

Everything here was Indian, for this place was Taos. It was the beginning of summer.

Little Taos boys live in Taos in summer.

THE CONVERSION OF A DOZEN YOUNG HOPIS

The students mentioned in the following article left for their homes last July. Letters have been received from all of them, and the reports show that they are making excellent use of their education. One has opened a small store, several are employed at their mechanical trades, one is engaged in a trader's store, and the rest are farming. A fine spirit of service to their people is breathed in their letters, which show their emancipation from paganism and the old life of opposition to progress and education.

That a misunderstanding of the white man's motives has been one of the causes of the Indian's backwardness in adopting civilized methods and of fighting education is being demonstrated at the Government Indian School at Carlisle, Pa., where twelve members of the Hopi nation, sun worshipers and pagans, who went there five years ago virtually as prisoners of war, are now preparing to spread the doctrine of the new life which they have gladly accepted.

These twelve Hopi Indians, when they arrived there five years ago, were crude specimens. Long hair hung down their backs, they were garbed in discarded khaki uniforms and blue army overcoats, and none of them could speak a word of English. Now these same Indians, having gone through the white man's melting pot, are considered among the best students in the school, have renounced the sun and have joined

---

(Excerpt from the *New York American,* October 1912 issue)

Christian churches, are precise gentlemen in their conduct, and one of them has achieved an international fame.

A half dozen years ago the Hopi nation was causing considerable trouble in Arizona. Internecine strife had divided the tribes, and a troop of United States cavalry was sent post haste to the Keam's Canyon region to restore peace.

After pow-wows and conferences in which the Indian leaders sternly refused to adopt the white man's education, twelve of the most obstinate "stand patters" were taken as prisoners of war and sent from the Moqui Agency in Arizona to the Carlisle Indian School, the party arriving there January 26, 1907. All of these Indians were members of the Oraibi band of the Hopi nation. Among them were several priests and head men of the tribe.

When these savages arrived at the Carlisle School they would have nothing to do with any of the other students and began to live their lives apart. As they could speak no English, they expressed their thoughts by gestures and in garbled language.

In order to experiment, the authorities of the school did not order these Hopis to have their long locks of hair cut, but waited to see if their association with the advanced Indians at the school would not have some good effect upon them. In less than ten days one of the Hopis indicated by gestures that he would like to have his hair cut like the other students, and on the same day another Hopi was discovered snipping off his own locks with a hunting knife.

From the moment the Hopis showed their first interest in eduation they advanced rapidly and became eager in their desire to learn more. They entered the lowest grades in the classrooms, but as they were attentive to their studies, were kindly disposed to their teachers, and caused not the slightest trouble, they climbed to the top. All were assigned to devote some portion of their time to vocational training, some entering the blacksmith shops or carpenter shops, and Lewis Tewanima, the crack Marathon runner, developed into an expert tailor.

"These boys were ridiculed at first by the other students, it being a common habit of the aboriginal race," declared Superintendent Friedman. "But the newcomers persevered, until they were among the most respected and best-liked students in the school. The Hopis were absolutely converted to education and civilization. Where before they were sun worshipers and the snake dance was one of their principal ceremonies, they have all joined Christian churches.

"When these Hopi boys return home they will be leaders among their people and fight for both education and righteousness. Now all speak English, all read and write, they are courteous, and are gentlemen. They have kept in continual touch with their people and already this influence has been noticeable in the Hopi country."

Lewis Tewanima, one of these same savages five years ago, is today the greatest long-distance runner in the world, and two years ago, while representing America at the Olympic games in Paris, won the main Marathon event. He represented this country at the recent Olympic games at Stockholm. Washington Talyumptewa has also achieved a national reputation as a long-distance runner.

LITTLE TAOS BOY
AT A DANCE

At the campfire supper there was buffalo meat and bread and coffee for everyone. Tso'u had not tasted buffalo meat before, but he knew how it should taste. His grandfather had told him. He said to the man at the barbecue pit, "I would like the meat from the hump part. It is sweeter there." All the Indians laughed. Even Pachole laughed. Tso'u did not like it. He took his bread and meat and sat within the shadows.

(Excerpt from Ann Clark, *Little Boy with Three Names,* Bureau of Indian Affairs, Chilocco, Oklahoma, 1940)

After the Indians had eaten they made ready for dancing. Pachole rebound his long hair, and Tso'u made his in a war-like roach as his grandfather had taught him to do it. They put on their arm feathers and their fan-tail feathers. They put on their dance moccasins. They got their willow hoops and Uncle's drum.

Then they joined the long, long line of Indians. Those who lived nearer and had come on horseback were at the head of the line. They rode their horses forward, slowly. Slowly they rode them into the great oval plaza of the Indian Ceremonial grounds. Slowly they walked them around the plaza and out again into the soft blackness of the night shadows. Then the line of men on foot moved forward. They moved forward into the Ceremonial plaza. There three of the biggest campfires that Tso'u had ever seen were burning. Their great logs crackled and blazed, sending showers of little sparks up into the night sky. All the tribes of Indians were singing their own songs. Some men made little dancing steps and other men stepped high into the light of the fire flames.

At the front side of the dancing space there were seats. They were high like the houses of Taos. Many people were sitting there. You could see their faces in the darkness. You could hear their hands moving. You could feel their eyes looking at you. You could feel them liking you.

At the back of the dancing space were the standing Indians and their horses and their wagons and their shelters and their campfires.

The stars were crowded close together and they were hanging low.

The line moved on before the seats of the people. Tso'u made dancing steps. He was not afraid. He could feel his heartbeats in his fingers and in his toes. He knew that his arm feathers and his fan-tail feathers were shining in the firelight. He whispered to Pachole, "I am riding White Pony over the high places. The clouds are at my feet. Rain falls below me."

Now all the Indians were in the Ceremonial dancing plaza.

They stopped walking. They grouped themselves at the back of the plaza. Then the different tribes danced their dances. Their chorus of singers sang for them and made them music with their rattles and drums and little bells.

Tso'u watched. He liked it.

Soon it was time for Taos dancing. All the faces out in the darkness were looking. The campfires flamed. Uncle sang the hoop dance song. Pachole and Tso'u danced. They turned their hoops this way and that way and made their bodies go through them, like the music of Uncle's singing. They made their bodies like water, pouring through the hoops in a flashing stream. They stepped lightly, lifting their feet as the words of the song lifted high in the air.

Then it was finished. The hoop dance was finished. All the dances were finished.

The Indians went back to their campfires. Tired ones went to sleep in their blankets, but the old ones sang the stars to bed and the sun to a new day.

For three days and three nights the Indians sang and danced and feasted together. On the morning of the fourth day the Ceremonial was over.

The Indians went back to their homes. On horseback and in wagons, in cars, on trains and buses, the Indians went home.

Ceremonial was over.

A 1950s CHILD OF THE SUN

As a girl named Beverly, listening to lectures in school delivered by teacher-nuns, I hardly felt like a "child of the Sun." But at home, less than a hundred years separated me from grandmothers and grandfathers who lived nothing but the wilderness life, in direct communication with the Sun. The influence of their ways was still very strong in the social life of our tribe, and important to the ways we children were raised.

Before I started going to boarding school, I lived with my

parents and six brothers in a one-room log house. We were lucky by then; when my oldest brothers were young, the family home was only a canvas tent, even when it went down to 40-below and prairie blizzards were howling! My parents worked hard at ranching, farming, and odd jobs, because they wanted to improve our situation.

Of course, we were not often alone in our family "mansion"; most of the time we had friends or relatives staying with us, as well. They often came from other reservations or from distant parts of our own, frequently traveling by horse and wagon. It was only natural, to us, that they should sleep over and share in our meals. Often they would stay for a couple of days, a week, or even longer.

You can imagine that we kids played outside a lot! The situation was not much different from life in a tipi, with the daytime household left mainly for adults. We always had lots of horses around the place, and riding them was as common as bike riding is for city kids. In the winter we spent a lot of time sliding down the hills near our home. Instead of having sleds made of buffalo ribs, or sitting on smooth buffalo hides, we used the hood of an old car. Our childhood chatterings were practically all still done in the language of our ancestors, as well.

There are two things I recall most about having other people staying in our house, the storytelling and the teasing. The first of these I enjoyed immensely, but the other one I always dreaded. Being the only daughter in the family made me the target of a lot of jokes about getting married. Somebody was always saying they had the ideal husband for me, and usually they referred to someone I thought was creepy or who looked scruffy. Besides, as a little girl I sure didn't want to get married!

An older cousin of ours was especially bad for this. Every time he came around, he'd say something like, "Hey, Beverly, you're going to get married the real Indian way, and I will be the one to choose your husband!" Sometimes he would come and say, "It is time for me to bring you to your husband."

Then I would run to my mother and hide. I knew that our
people had such a custom—that a father or brother could
choose a husband for a young girl—so I always thought this
cousin might be serious.

One time he happened to be in our house while I was
showing off my first sewing. This was still before I started
going to school. "Oh, this is very good," he said right out, "now
that you know how to sew, you are ready to come meet your
husband. You better go and pack your suitcase and things."
Instead of bringing me to a husband, he just brought me to
tears instead.

I don't remember being spanked by my parents or ever getting a beating. I do recall my mother telling me to be careful,
that if I didn't listen to what I was told, my uncle would get
mad at me or, worse, a coyote would come and bite me. Uncles
were often disciplinarians, and I have gotten a few stern lectures from mine.

We didn't go to town very often, so for me it was always a
special treat. I got a lot of warnings on the way, and I always
stayed very close to my mother. I was raised as a girl, in a society with strict divisions between boys and girls. This sometimes made life hard for me, in a family full of boys. Often they
would get to go places and do things when I wasn't allowed. I
used to resent this, though I understand much better now.

In those days before television, we used to have a lot of
family entertainment, especially in the evenings, and if there
were visitors. A lot of Indians taught themselves to play instru-
ments. Maybe they didn't sound quite like the records we
heard on radio, but they played our favorite tunes, and we
could all join in. In our household, my father and brothers
played guitar, their favorite tunes being Western and gospel.
However, they would be just as likely to bring out a drum to sit
around and strike a beat in company to traditional Indian
songs.

But the favorite entertainment of all was storytelling, and
this was done best by our family elders, who knew all kinds of

A girl of the Ute tribe is seen taking care of her little brother or sister in the early 1870s, when they and their people still lived wild and free. This style of cradleboard was common among several tribes. One feature that varied from place to place was the face guard and shelter, from plain buckskin visors to sturdy wooden hoops fully decorated with beads. Beadwork designs on the large headboards often indicated which tribe it came from.

Two Salish-Flathead boys and a girl at a powwow dance in Arlee, Montana, about 1907. Partly because they welcomed missionaries into their country so early, these people found less outside interference into cultural activities during the early 1900s, when other tribes had a far greater struggle. Dances were held frequently, and parents usually took their children, everyone in costume and speaking the native language. The boys here are wearing headdresses made from porcupine hair, which bounce with each breeze and dance movement. Their braids are decorated with otter-fur wraps, and one wears a sash of the same kind. The girl has a wool dress, edged with ribbon and embroidered with a beaded yoke, from which strings of beads and shells are suspended. Like her mother and grandmothers, she wears a contrasting cloth blouse under her dress. Some Flathead women wore four or five capes, blouses, skirts, and dresses at the same time, all of different patterned material and worn so that some parts of each were visible. This created a very colorful image, which Flathead children eagerly took up, and sometimes still do.

Modern Children of the Sun! Two Crowshoe boys—Jason and his cousin Ira—pause from riding their contemporary "bronco." Jason's parents just finished hosting a very sacred traditional ceremony in the two tipis at the rear, in which the boys took part. The boots and chaps are proof that Jason rides real horses, too. The scene is on the Piegan Reserve of Southern Alberta in 1983.

Three of our boys and their great-grandmother at our Rocky Mountain home. From left to right: Okan, Anadaki (or Hilda Strangling Wolf), Wolf, and Iniskim.

Our daughter, Star, resting peacefully in her swing, where she spent a lot of time safe and out of the way in our small and crowded household. In the long ago, Star's "grandmothers" would have made this swing with a tanned deer or elk skin suspended by rawhide cords tied between two tipi poles. Hers was simply made with a quilt and some clothesline rope tied to two large nails firmly anchored in a ceiling-support beam. The quilt is folded so that her own weight holds it together. One light push made it swing for some time, and this action invariably put her to sleep after she was changed and fed.

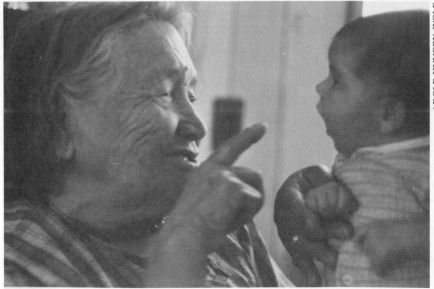

Anadaki (Pretty Woman) beams with delight as she meets the latest great-granddaughter, Star, come for a visit from across the mountains. Anadaki was saying, "It's been close to a hundred years since I was tiny like you!"

The old chief and his grandsons. Cultural activities, such as this powwow dance at the foot of the Canadian Rockies in 1983, have helped many Indian elders pass on the spirit of outdoor life and adventures to younger generations. Many families spend their summers on the "powwow circuit," traveling from one tribal camp to the next, contemporary nomads on the trails of their ancestors—even if pickup trucks and travel trailers have replaced horses and tipis.

Enjoying the deep snow and cold weather of wintertime. Okan and Star (*left*) are using snowshoes to get around in the waist-deep powder, while Iniskim prefers to slide down the hills on small skis. Wolf is looking out from a snowhouse they all built and used until it eventually melted. Real outdoor kids don't think of winter as a time of suffering from cold weather and staying indoors. Outdoor life makes them hardy and enables them to appreciate the pleasant weather of summer all the more. It also gives them more reason to help celebrate the traditional end-of-winter ceremonials, which some tribes still hold.

The Hungry Wolf boys (Iniskim and Wolf at left, Okan at right) learn to entertain visitors from the States with an "intertribal" powwow dance, as their forefathers might have done. The occasion was the summer of 1976, when Shota and Sage Burkhart came to our camp in the Canadian Rockies with their parents. Elaborate pieces of children's costumes, such as fully-beaded vests, belts, and moccasins, are often passed down as family heirlooms. Art dealers and relic collectors have caused mayhem to this system by offering tempting amounts of cash. It takes strong-willed parents to ignore these temptations, especially if the cupboards are fairly empty of food and a nearby trunk holds family relics whose next users have not yet shown themselves.

Participation is the traditional Indian way for children to learn adult life. Here two mothers (*left*) work with three boys to cut up a moose carcass, dropped off that morning by one of the tribe's hunters for those staying at a ceremonial encampment along an isolated river bottom in Southern Alberta, in 1981. One of the first things modern kids often learn with this kind of work is not to say "oooohh!" and "yuck!" while getting their hands and arms coated with blood and guts. Another is to appreciate natural foods, and how to handle them!

This traditional version of bicycle and tricycle was being used by Iniskim, Okan, and Star during a ceremonial encampment near the Canadian Rockies, in 1981. Children among horse-using tribes in the old days usually grew up without any fear of the animals. While family horse herds grazed some distance from camp, most households kept a gentle colt or mare nearby, one that would not kick or act up even if a child crawled under it or hung onto its legs. Infants were sometimes tied on such a horse's back and allowed to sleep there.

Okan and Iniskim set up their own little tipi next to our large family lodge. The poles must be placed properly, over a good foundation, and tied at the right height if the cover is to look neat and function correctly.

Satisfied that the poles are all in place, the two boys lift up the main pole, to which is tied the canvas cover. Campers who think tipis are difficult to use will be surprised to see that two boys (then aged about seven and eight) can perform the task quite easily.

On this occasion everything worked out well, so the boys pin the covers together with willow sticks that they just finished cutting. They had a great time entertaining young visitors inside their small lodge, thus leaving the main tipis mainly for the adults.

The boys stretch their tipi cover around the pole framework. If they don't set this up right, the cover either won't reach or will end up hanging too loosely. However, a fair amount of adjustment is possible afterward by moving the poles farther in or out.

Okan and Iniskim enjoying a simple form of "tipi life" that kids anywhere could make. They gathered a few poles, tied them together to make a sort of frame, then covered that with some old quilts and blankets (notice the hole through one of them!). The boys have raided their mom's supply of dried meat, nuts, and raisins, and are pretending they've just prepared a tipi meal.

A traditional children's home in the Canadian Rockies, autumn 1983. This little tipi has since been replaced by two others, for which the kids received ceremonial designs handed down from family elders. With the designs came certain rules of behavior in and around the lodges, which will help prepare their young occupants for adult life within the disciplined tribal culture. From left: Wolf, Okan, Iniskim, and sister Star.

Outdoor life for little children, winter 1973. Wolf and Okan were well dressed in fur hats and wrapped with warm quilts and blankets as we took them for a ride through the frozen wilderness of our home, nestled in a wooden box fastened on top of a wooden toboggan.

Right, Okan clowns with his brothers during a break in powwow dancing one summer evening. Two braids at the side and one down the back is a traditional style for Blackfoot boys, and for younger men heading out on the warpath. Girls and women wear only two braids (or leave their hair loose) with a part down the middle, whereas Blackfoot men wearing only two braids keep the part to one side or wear the center of their hair in some style of forelock. Missionary schools made strong efforts to wipe out long-hair styles, but recent generations have revived their popularity.

Our son Iniskim, age six, standing outside our family tipi, ready for a summer evening powwow dance, much as his great-grandfather might have done. It is gratifying that predictions from the early 1900s of the "Vanishing Indian" have not proved true. Not only are native cultural events still blossoming, they are even taught in the once-strict reservation schools.

Among noted Sun Dance leaders in the Blackfeet Tribe of Montana was the former warrior Swims Under, seen here in about 1920 with his son Mike. The two are dressed and ready for a tribal celebration. Like his dad, young Mike wears a weasel-skin decorated shirt, which was transferred to him during a special ritual. In former times such shirts gave prestige and spiritual power to men on warpaths and at peace treaties. The eagle-feather headdresses were also transferred during rituals.

Now himself a tribal elder and leader of the Blackfoot Sun Dance, along with other sacred ceremonies, Mike Swims Under is seen here with Star and Iniskim while visiting our mountain home in the fall of 1985 and sharing some of his wisdom. Mike was about seventy-two.

tribal legends and lore. On my father's side, especially, there were many brave warriors, so my father's uncles often came and talked about them.

Our favorite uncle was Jack Low Horn, who was more like our grandpa, especially since my dad's father died long before any of us kids were born. Jack lived about three miles across the prairie from us, as the crow flies. Sometimes when we saw him walking across the fields toward our home, we would run out to meet him.

My youngest brother, Gary, was Jack Low Horn's favorite, I guess because he was just a little boy of two or three.

They were really fond of each other, the old man and the little boy. I remember the last time they saw each other, and it was sure sad. Jack had TB and spent his final months in a sanitarium in Calgary. We all went to see him, but only our parents were allowed to go inside. Jack came to the window and put his hand where my little brother was holding his, then the old man started to cry, and pretty soon they were both crying.

Unfortunately, at this time the missionaries still had a strong hold on the lives of Indian people, so I was forced to leave home at the age of six and move into our reserve's Catholic-run boarding school. Life sure became lonesome for me then. Nowadays I feel strongly against any system that takes children away from their parents and forces them to learn whatever *they* teach.

In my case, I learned from the nuns to be ashamed for being a "child of the Sun," though the term they used was more like a "little heathen," or a child born of pagan people. They soon convinced my young mind that our tribal culture was uncouth and that our people were too savage to have a "religion." They kept us all in line with constant fears of venial and mortal sins. We understood that all people are liable to sin, but Indians even more so.

One reason I was lonely at boarding school was that we each had to sleep on a separate bed and keep ourselves very private from each other, even though there were sometimes over one hundred girls in our dormitory. We showered with robes on, and heaven help the one who should make an out-of-the-way joke! Even the time we spent alone in the bathroom was measured, as were the pieces of toilet paper we were given!

Sometimes we got to see movies at the school, and one time it was a scary movie. I woke up during the middle of that night with bad dreams from it. I sat up in my bed and tried to calm myself down. Then I heard the girl below me calling my name, and it turned out she couldn't sleep for the same reason, so I went down and we kept each other company. Besides the movie, we were also afraid because a storm was making the doors and windows of our building rattle.

Because we woke up during the night, we overslept the next morning. I suddenly found myself awake as a nun was dragging me from the bed by my hair. She slapped my face and said things to make me feel guilty in front of the others, all because I'd been too scared to sleep alone. In our crowded home, I seldom had the luxury of a bed to myself, but here it was a great sin to sleep next to another.

The kids who had it worst in school were those from traditional families, ones who were even more "children of the Sun" in their first years than I. By the time I got to school, I had learned a little English, but these kids usually spoke none. That made things tough, in a place where speaking our Indian language was instantly punished.

Even worse, kids in our school who came from traditional families had to carry a burden of guilt, because their parents usually had medicine bundles and took part in tribal religious ceremonies. Those were "heathen practices," so the nuns would work extra hard to "save" these kids from damnation. Of course, we picked up on these attitudes and became critical of our own ancestral ways. We didn't want to be seen with our elderly relatives, especially if they were old-time Indians with braids and moccasins. In those days there were still quite a few such people in the tribe, including some in our own family.

There was always a lot of commotion when school classes began for the year, as parents brought their children to board for the year away from home. It was so sad that as a little girl I always cried. Some kids would run after their parents as they drove away, often in wagons. An older brother or sister would have to hold them back, or one of the nuns would drag them up the stairs and into the school. Indian life is a family life, and it disrupted our society greatly when these missionaries forced all children at age six to leave home.

When I got older, I sometimes found the new arrivals at school funny, after they got over the first emotional scenes. Many were very ignorant of "white ways," especially those who came from traditional households. A lot of these kids spoke no English, or just a little that they picked up from older kids around their households. Imagine these children trying to understand the English spoken by our nuns, who were mostly French-speaking Catholics! No wonder you can recognize from which tribe or reserve many Indian children come, by the unusual pronunciations of their English.

I suppose a lot of things at first amazed me about these so-called white ways at our boarding school, but none more so than the strict rules of bathroom use. We were only allowed to go at certain times of the day, and I've already mentioned that toilet paper was rationed out to us. Three pieces was the standard rule. It all seemed so unnatural to me, and it still does. I suspect all of you agree with me, so I mention this not as a complaint against non-Indian society, but rather so that you can get a better understanding why Indian people have so often felt they were torn from their own culture.

Near the end of one school year I got vaccinated for something, and this made me quite sick; my arm really swelled up, and I couldn't attend classes. The principal told my parents they could take me home. At this time they happened to be camping in the Rocky Mountains, on a special part of the Blood Indian Reserve that we received by treaty so that we'd have a good source of logs for building and ranching. My parents were there with several other families, whose men were all cutting wood.

When I first got to this camp, I got even sicker, because I

wasn't used to the rugged and simple life-style. The food was mostly bread, potatoes, and meat, which the men hunted nearby. We were just a few miles from the edge of Waterton National Park, as well as Glacier National Park, which begins at the U.S. border. I think the hunters shot mostly elk, but there were also deer and moose nearby.

I didn't really like this "wild life" at first; it seemed too close to the "primitive ways" that the nuns were always deriding. But with fresh air and sunshine, plus the nearness and attention of my mother and other kind women, I quickly got back into the flow of my first years. That feeling was probably helped along even further by evening story sessions, and drumming songs, which brought back the pride I'd always felt around the elders of our family. I was still young enough to let the newly learned biases against Indian life slip back out of my life, at least for a while.

I recall a funny incident that shows how ignorant I was of real traditional living. One night the dogs in our camp barked really ferociously, and there was a lot of noise in a shed that the men had built for storage of meat, harnesses, and other things. Of course, there were a lot of bears in this region from the nearby parks, though I didn't know much about this. There were both blacks and grizzlies, and still are today.

The next morning when the men checked their shed, they found a bunch of stuff missing, mostly the stored belongings of a family that had gone down the mountain for a few days. After the men went to work, I played down at the creek that ran past the camp for a while. When I got bored with that, I went off down a trail, "exploring." Pretty soon I found the missing stuff, or at least most of it. When the men came back from work and found out, they really praised me.

My uncle was there, and he was especially proud of me. "My, you are a brave girl," he said, "to wander down these trails without ever fearing that a bear would grab you." Heck no, I though to myself, I wasn't afraid—I'd never even thought about it. Boy, was I scared about it afterward! But at the time I was really proud of my uncle's praise—it went a long way for me. Of course, I didn't brag about this primitive adventure when I finally got back to boarding school that fall.

One of my favorite entertainments when I was around home was to visit my great-aunt and get her to tell stories. I often went there with one of my cousins, who was also her granddaughter, and we both usually brought our little brothers, who were at the same age. This old lady was an invalid, so she seldom went away from home. Since she lived out in the country, she was usually glad for our company. We would all lie on her bed together, while she kept us excited and spellbound. Her name was Calling Two Ways, and she was married to my mom's uncle, Joe Heavy Head.

The way she treated us was the custom among our old people. I think extended-family members did more of the child raising, in former times, than did the parents themselves. It was a busy life back then, from morning till night, keeping a household going in a tipi. But the old folks usually sat around and had time and patience for the little ones. Imagine how different was the education kids got, coming as it did from people who had to be somewhat wise about life just to have survived into old age. Today, teachers of the young are often people still struggling to learn how to live themselves.

Family elders like these lived in their own tipi as long as they were able. It was not unusual for kids to spend more time there than in the lodge of their own parents, or even to make their permanent beds in the old folks' place. This was handy, among other things, since there was usually more visiting and traffic in the main family lodge. Thus space there was at a premium, whereas the old people were glad to have someone nearby who would fetch them such things as wood and water.

It was also common for kids to spend a lot of time with an aunt and uncle's family, with the family of a best friend, or even with a couple who was unrelated but had taken a liking to the young one. Adoption in Indian life was generally a pretty simple process whereby a young person might just slowly find himself living somewhere other than his original home. Parents generally had the attitude that a child should go wherever he or she finds most happiness. Of course, since everyone usually lived in the same camp circle, the physical separation didn't really amount to much.

However, there are also many stories of young kids being adopted by people from other tribes, or from distant divisions of their own tribes. A husband and wife who lost a child might see another that reminded them of the lost one. They might ask the parents for the child, even if they were from far away. Whenever possible, the parents let them adopt this look-alike, or whatever, and if the child was willing, they'd let him or her move away with them. Such children were generally treated exceptionally well by their adoptive parents.

There are also numerous stories of children leaving their own tribes to find new homes among another people. Sometimes this was because their parents had died, perhaps had been killed. Orphans usually found places to live among their own relatives, but they were often placed behind the family's own kids in the pecking order, meaning they had to do the hardest chores or got the least attention.

My own father had some unpleasant experiences as an orphan. His dad—my grandfather, Robert Little Bear—died when my dad was only three, during the influenza epidemic around 1918, when, incidentally, many Indian people died. Thereafter, my grandmother remarried to a noted man in the tribe who already had a large family. His wife had also died, but his aged mother lived with him and looked after the children. Neither this man nor his mother cared much for the new woman's kids, including my dad. He was made to sleep on the floor, his bed being a piece of cardboard and an old coat, with another coat to cover him. The man's own children slept together in proper beds. In the mornings they were allowed to stay in bed, while my dad was chased outside to look after the horses. Sometimes the old woman made special treats for the kids, but when my dad tried to get some, she only gave him a dirty look or made mean faces at him.

The house where his family lived was along the road into town, so that other relatives frequently dropped in for short visits. One day my father's uncle, Willie Eagle Plume, stopped by to see his sister and her kids in their new environment. When he got ready to leave, he found my dad crying, begging to go with him. He learned of the mistreatment, so without much ado he went back to the home and advised everyone that he was taking my dad along with him. No one objected, and from then on this uncle was like a father to my dad.

Ironically, on my mother's side of the family just about the opposite thing happened. In the late buffalo days my mom's grandmother married a German immigrant named Joseph Trollinger, with whom she had a number of children. They all lived in a big house some distance from our tribe's reserve, where they operated a stage stop and restaurant.

One of these kids was deaf, so Trollinger decided to bring him to Germany for medical treatment. When my great-grandmother learned of his plans, she packed up all the kids and moved back to her own people. She was pregnant at that time with my grandmother, Anadaki, or Pretty Woman. Within a few months she remarried, this time to a young warrior and future medicine man named Heavy Head, who was unable to father any children. He not only took my grandmother as his own, after she was born, but he also treated the other children with much kindness and respect. My mother said it was a long time before she realized this man wasn't her real grandfather, because he showed so much affection for his grandkids when they started coming along.

This Heavy Head did a lot of traditional doctoring when he got older, and my great-grandmother helped him with it. Although we've had our own Indian hospital in town since the time my mother was young, it was still common for people to call on our traditional medicine men when I was growing up. In spite of all the critical comments made by nuns and other missionaries, I think most everyone in the tribe had some faith still in the old, natural ways of doctoring.

However, this reminds me of a story that always gets some

laughs in my family. One of my older brothers was sickly while young, and he used to get doctored by our great-grandfather, Heavy Head. I cannot tell you the process, which the old man learned through a combination of dreams and firsthand experience, but I know it involved a lot of praying and singing—to the accompaniment of drums—in addition to herbal brews and physical treatments.

My brother used to have frequent seizures as part of his ailment, and my mother had learned to keep a tub of mustard water on hand for this purpose. So, one time while this old man was doing his doctoring, my brother got another of his spells. Heavy Head didn't notice, because his eyes were closed while he was singing and praying. My mom grabbed her little boy from where he lay before the doctor, and she rushed him to the mustard water, which quickly eased the convulsions. The humor comes from the way my mother describes the look on the old man's face when he finished singing, opened his eyes, and found that his little patient had disappeared.

My mother was never an Indian doctor, although some women were, but she treated a lot of our childhood ailments with what would now be called folk remedies. Some of these were of native origin, others were learned from non-Indian neighbors and from health care workers. In the times when few of our people had motor vehicles, families who had medical problems often moved into town and camped outside the Indian hospital, usually in tents, so that the sick ones could be close to medical help. This was also done for expectant mothers after the government discouraged traditional midwifery.

Like schoolkids everywhere, the time I looked forward to most every year was summer vacation, because then we got to live back home and relax, "let our hair down," so to speak. Thank heavens I didn't grow up in my parents' time, when they even had to spend most of the summer at school.

Summer in Indian country means time for dance pow-wows, tipi camps, and the sacred Sun Dance celebrations. Kids from traditional families could expect to spend much of their time camped in tipis, eating food cooked outdoors, and meeting other traditional people. Sometimes problems with the young came up because they no longer understood the customs of their people, or else no longer had respect for them because of influence from nuns in school. Elders began to shake their heads when they looked outside their tipis and saw their grandchildren "hanging around," talking a new language, and caring not for the simple and natural ways handed down.

Ours wasn't a traditional family, so we didn't spend too much time at tipi encampments. But when we did go there, our parents always warned us about certain things that were forbidden, such as throwing stones at tipis or going near any medicine bundle. If there was a sacred ceremony going on, we were usually chased away so that we wouldn't cause any harm, we were told. The elders knew that we were being brainwashed at school to look down on the old ways, and for some reason they chose not to make an effort at holding us back. I guess this is because in the Indian way there is no religious missionizing, though I wish our old folks had thought of some ways to keep us nearer at hand when they were practicing our tribal culture.

A SUN DANCE CHILD
OF THE BLACKFEET

My name is Mike Swims Under. My parents called me Many Stars, which is my Indian name. My father's name was Swims Under, but he was also called Chief Bird and Last Tail Feather. My mother's name was Mink Woman. She was a Holy Woman; she put up Sun Dance Lodges with my father. I grew up in the Sun Dances with them.

The first thing I remember about my parents is how devoted they were to our Blackfoot traditional customs and religion; they raised me to be devoted to them, as well. They

(Told by tribal elder Mike Swims Under in our home in fall 1985)

brought me along to all the many ceremonies, including the Beaver Bundle and Medicine Pipe Dances, in addition to the Sun Lodge, which was the biggest event of all.

In Blackfoot we say *minipoka* to a child who is treated like I was, one who is taken to ceremonies among the tribe's leaders. In this way I learned to respect the customs of my ancestors. I learned the songs and the ways of praying. I learned to love Nature and the Sun.

Life has changed a great deal on the Blackfeet Reservation since I was born, in 1913. But it changed a great deal in the time of my parents, too. My father was born before our people settled down; they were still living with the buffalo, which was a much different kind of life than we have now.

My father taught me the disciplines of our ceremonial ways, and there are many. I was given initiations so that I could take part. He warned me never to practice any of these ceremonials, or even sing their songs, unless I first got initiated. He said it would be harmful if I just made up ceremonial things out of my own mind. Such things as songs, face paintings, and so forth, these have all been handed down from dreams and visions of various people. They are not just made up or imitated for style and show!

I was able to grow because of the breast. My mother fed me, and this was the way she gave me nourishment. She gave me part of herself. That is how it goes in nature; the children are fed from the bodies of their mothers.

When I got bigger, I remember receiving broths. That is how I was introduced to adult food. I also recall eating from the collection of fine crumbs that collected at the bottoms of my mother's rawhide parfleches. In them she stored dried meat, berries, fat, dried roots, and mint. This mixture was my childhood delicacy.

My mother and father never whipped me, or even spanked me. They spoke sternly to me, and lectured me often, starting when I got old enough to reason. All the time that I grew up they kept after me, and that is how I turned out to be who I am.

I didn't always listen to my parents as I grew older. The time came when I started smoking, then drinking moonshine liquor. My parents always told me what the consequences of my actions could do to my life. But they never hit me. I finally gave up drinking, when I saw that it kept me from enjoying my life and my prayers fully.

Now I work instead to help the people of our tribe, by setting an example in the Sun Lodge. There are enough initiated people so that we can still carry on with it, and some of them are quite young. I am now the leader for the ceremonies, and I try to do just what my father did when he was leader. It is sometimes very difficult for me, because there are no elders left with whom I can consult. My parents did not have this problem, but I am still doing my best.

When my parents were still children, everyone in the tribe took part in the Sun Dance, or Okan, and everybody believed in it. They all knew how to behave there, with respect.

It was still quite a bit like this when I grew up, although not so many people took a direct part anymore. Not so many learned the songs and got the initiations. The camps kept getting smaller, until finally we thought the Sun Dance and everything with it was going to end forever.

But now there are again many younger people who show faith in these ways. For a long time it was only old people, but now the young have come part of the way back to our own ways. They are at least trying to keep some of our ceremonies going. It should be up to the parents to teach their children about our customs; about the many rules and regulations. But most parents today don't know much about it, so some of the young people have a hard time to get good advice. The main thing is to have respect for all things, and lots of patience. You have to treat our way of life good, if you want it to help you.

Prayers, songs, and incense are powerful things to live on; they give you courage and good luck. Now that I am old, I can fully understand what my mother and father tried to tell me about faith and goodness. I'm following my ancestors, and I consider my life a holy way. I give thanks to the Sun and the Earth for letting me live. I give thanks for the Sunny Days and the Cloudy Days. I think all true prayers go to the same creator. . . .

I encourage the young people to learn about the ways of their ancestors—the ways of living with respect for nature. It is easy nowadays, even the schools encourage it. In my time this was not so; the society of my time did not encourage us to be like Indians. In some of the mission schools they beat kids who showed interest in our customs, or who spoke the Indian language. They cut their hair right off, and tried to make white children out of them.

I was lucky, I didn't go to a mission school. My parents wanted me nearby them, so my father would not let me be taken away to boarding school. I attended a small day school near our home, instead. I have always lived close to the mountains, on our reservation, far from the towns.

Our school had ordinary government teachers, instead of nuns and priests, so things were more relaxed. My parents rented one of the little houses by the school, so they even lived near me in the daytime. Several families lived around there like that. It was somewhat like the old-time camps, except that we got government rations instead of having to follow the buffalo. Even so, my father did hunt for some of our meat, which my mother prepared in the old ways. We also grew a vegetable garden, which they learned to do from the white people. I have grown gardens for most of my life.

I am saddened when I see how many children today grow up in a very crazy life. Even their parents don't set good examples for them. Many don't care for their children, only for themselves. They hit their children and neglect them. The old people used to say, "When you hit a child, you knock them crazy." The more you hit them, it seems, the crazier they get.

But nowadays there are children who don't get any discipline at all, not just hitting, and they are just as crazy. They only watch TV, and they copy what they see on it. Or they copy other kids who have copied the TV. It's all crazy, and it makes no sense to me. There is no prayer and no purpose to it. I'm glad whenever I see some of them returning to the ways of faith and prayer. Faith in life is what I've gotten from the ways that my parents taught to me.

CHAPTER SEVEN

Tales for the Fireside

Children of the Sun loved to hear stories by the fireside. In their simple, nature-oriented lives, storytelling was a major form of entertainment, not to mention *the* means for passing on tribal history, culture, and beliefs. Storytelling sessions were as important to traditional outdoor life as classroom lectures are in modern schoolrooms.

Children who showed early signs of learning the myths and tales of their ancestors were pointed out, by elders, as ones most likely to succeed in life. Noted storytellers were usually wise and creative, with much knowledge of medical and mystical things. They were skilled at relieving childhood ailments in several different ways. Yet, some of them were just plain good talkers.

In contrast, members of the Blackfoot Confederacy (including Beverly's Blood people) have inherited such a complex body of tribal lore that numerous persons must work together to maintain different parts of it. Elaborate legends combine with lengthy rituals, prayers, and songs to produce ceremonial dramas that highlight the history of Blackfoot traditional life.

Beverly grew up among some of the elders involved in that

particular legendary complex. Until boarding-school influence distracted her from it, she thought that every important thing in life was explained in the stories these elders told. It confused her when the nuns at school later said the fireside tales of her ancestors were pagan nonsense, but that the equally mystical stories of *their* Bible were truth.

Although the nuns managed to make her feel ashamed of the tribal heritage, Beverly still recalls childhood feelings of pride when her dad's old uncle flashed his gnarled hands through the air to punctuate the brave adventures of some family forebear or to describe the actions of some mystical being who once communed with members of the tribe.

Napi was the clown in tribal stories, the trickster and troublemaker. Yet, he was also involved in making the earth, working with what the elders called the Creator. In school she was told that the Creator is God, and the trickster is the devil. But in the elders' stories, Napi was a jovial sort of devil, with no hell for a home, nor did the Creator threaten anyone with everlasting punishment.

Fireside storytelling sessions serve to stimulate a child's mind and ambition. Even today children feel the magic of an open fire, as surely as all our ancestors felt it. What better time to tell stories and discuss the meaning of life? In the tribal past, legends introduced young listeners to dangers and hardships as challenges to overcome, goals to be proudly reached, rather than as fearful events to be dreaded. Can your children say that about the stories *they* hear, today?

Elders even gave their fireside listeners tests for courage. After a particularly hair-raising tale, an elder might ask a certain youngster to go out and fetch a pail of water. If there was a braggart or show-off in the bunch, he was sure to be chosen. Refusal meant ridicule in front of family and friends, so most kids bit their lips and rushed to the nearest source of water. Sometimes, if the elder felt the message had not been properly received yet by the child, he might spill out the water and say, "That was quick. Go get me some more!"

The stories we present here are but a few from the vast native collections that seem like the leaves of many trees. Fortunately, there are still native people committed to learning and passing on many of these tales, even with all the modern competition. Our selection is merely presented to encourage your thoughts on this subject and to hope that you'll take time out, now and then, to share tales and stories with the children who are around in your life.

MANITOSHAW,
THE HUNTING GIRL

It was in the winter, in the Moon of Difficulty (January). We had eaten our venison roast for supper, and the embers were burning brightly. Our teepee was especially cheerful. Uncheedah (my grandmother) sat near the entrance, my uncle and his wife upon the opposite side, while I with my pets occupied the remaining space.

Wabeda, the dog, lay near the fire in a half doze, watching out of the corners of his eyes the tame raccoon, which snuggled back against the walls of the teepee, his shrewd brain, doubtless, concocting some mischief for the hours of darkness. I had already recited a legend of our people. All agreed that I had done well. Having been so generously praised, I was eager to earn some more compliments by learning a new one, so I begged my uncle to tell me a story. Musingly he replied:

"I can give you a Sioux-Cree tradition," and immediately began:

"Many winters ago, there were six teepees standing on the southern slope of Moose mountain in the Moon of Wild Cherries (September). The men to whom these teepees belonged had been attacked by the Sioux while hunting buffalo, and

(Excerpt from Charles Alexander Eastman, *Indian Boyhood*, McClure, Phillips & Co., New York, 1902)

nearly all killed. Two or three who managed to get home to tell their sad story were mortally wounded, and died soon afterward. There was only one old man and several small boys left to hunt and provide for this unfortunate little band of women and children.

"They lived upon teepsinna (wild turnips) and berries for many days. They were almost famished for meat. The old man was too feeble to hunt successfully. One day in this desolate camp a young Cree maiden—for such they were—declared that she could no longer sit still and see her people suffer. She took down her dead father's second bow and quiver full of arrows, and begged her old grandmother to accompany her to Lake Wanagiska, where she knew that moose had oftentimes been found. I forgot to tell you that her name was Manitoshaw.

"This Manitoshaw and her old grandmother, Nawakewee, took each a pony and went far up into the woods on the side of the mountain. They pitched their wigwam just out of sight of the lake, and hobbled their ponies. Then the old woman said to Manitoshaw:

" 'Go, my granddaughter, to the outlet of the Wanagiska, and see if there are any moose tracks there. When I was a young woman, I came here with your father's father, and we pitched our tent near this spot. In the night there came three different moose. Bring me leaves of the birch and cedar twigs; I will make medicine for moose,' she added.

"Manitoshaw obediently disappeared in the woods. It was a grove of birch and willow, with two good springs. Down below was a marshy place. Nawakewee had bidden the maiden look for nibbled birch and willow twigs, for the moose loves to eat them, and to have her arrow ready upon the bowstring. I have seen this very place many a time," added my uncle, and this simple remark gave the story an air of reality.

"The Cree maiden went first to the spring, and there found fresh tracks of the animal she sought. She gathered some cedar berries and chewed them, and rubbed some of them on her garments so that the moose might not scent her. The sun was all ready to set, and she felt she must return to Nawakewee.

"Just then Hinhankaga, the hooting owl, gave his doleful night call. The girl stopped and listened attentively.

" 'I thought it was a lover's call,' she whispered to herself. A singular challenge pealed across the lake. She recognized the alarm call of the loon, and fancied that the bird might have caught a glimpse of her game.

"Soon she was within a few paces of the temporary lodge of pine boughs and ferns which the grandmother had constructed. The old woman met her on the trail.

" 'Ah, my child, you have returned none too soon. I feared you had ventured too far away; for the Sioux often come to this place to hunt. You must not expose yourself carelessly on the shore.'

"As the two women lay down to sleep they could hear the ponies munch the rich grass in an open spot nearby. Through the smoke hole of the pine-bough wigwam Manitoshaw gazed up into the starry sky, and dreamed of what she would do on the morrow when she should surprise the wily moose. Her grandmother was already sleeping so noisily that it was enough to scare away the game. At last the maiden, too, lost herself in sleep.

"Old Nawakewee awoke early. First of all she made a fire and burned cedar and birch so that the moose might not detect the human smell. Then she quickly prepared a meal of wild turnips and berries, and awoke the maiden, who was surprised to see that the sun was already up. She ran down to the spring and hastily splashed handsful of the cold water in her face; then she looked for a moment in its mirrorlike surface. There was the reflection of two moose by the open shore and beyond them Manitoshaw seemed to see a young man standing. In another moment all three had disappeared.

" 'What is the matter with my eyes? I am not fully awake yet, and I imagine things. Ugh, it is all in my eyes," the maiden repeated to herself. She hurried back to Nawakewee. The vision was so unexpected and so startling that she could not believe in its truth, and she said nothing to the old woman.

"Breakfast eaten, Manitoshaw threw off her robe and appeared in her scantily cut gown of buckskin with long fringes, and moccasins and leggings trimmed with quills of the porcupine. Her father's bow and quiver were thrown over one shoulder, and the knife dangled from her belt in its handsome sheath. She ran breathlessly along the shore toward the outlet.

"Way off near the island Medoza the loon swam with his mate, occasionally uttering a cry of joy. Here and there the playful Hogan, the trout, sprang gracefully out of the water, in a shower of falling dew. As the maiden hastened along she scared up Wadawasee, the kingfisher, who screamed loudly.

" 'Stop, Wadawasee, stop—you will frighten my game!'

"At last she had reached the outlet. She saw at once that the moose had been there during the night. They had torn up the ground and broken birch and willow twigs in a most disorderly way."

"Ah!" I exclaimed, "I wish I had been with Manitoshaw then!"

"Hush, my boy; never interrupt a storyteller."

I took a stick and began to level off the ashes in front of me, and to draw a map of the lake, the outlet, the moose and Manitoshaw. Away off to one side was the solitary wigwam, Nawakewee and the ponies.

"Manitoshaw's heart was beating so loud that she could not hear anything," resumed my uncle. "She took some leaves of the wintergreen and chewed them to calm herself. She did not forget to throw in passing a pinch of pulverized tobacco and paint into the spring for Manitou, the spirit.

"Among the twinkling leaves of the birch her eye was caught by a moving form, and then another. She stood motionless, grasping her heavy bow. The moose, not suspecting any danger, walked leisurely toward the spring. One was a large female moose; the other a yearling.

"As they passed Manitoshaw, moving so naturally and looking so harmless, she almost forgot to let fly an arrow. The mother moose seemed to look in her direction, but did not see her. They had fairly passed her hiding-place when she stepped forth and sent a swift arrow into the side of the larger moose. Both dashed into the thick woods, but it was too late. The Cree maiden had already loosened her second arrow. Both fell dead before reaching the shore."

"Uncle, she must have had a splendid aim, for in the woods the many little twigs make an arrow bound off to one side," I interrupted in great excitement.

"Yes, but you must remember she was very near the moose."

"It seems to me, then, uncle, that they must have scented her, for you have told me that they possess the keenest nose of any animal," I persisted.

"Doubtless the wind was blowing the other way. But, nephew, you must let me finish my story.

"Overjoyed by her success, the maiden hastened back to Nawakewee, but she was gone! The ponies were gone, too, and the wigwam of branches had been demolished. While Manitoshaw stood there, frightened and undecided what to do, a soft voice came from behind a neighboring thicket:

" 'Manitoshaw! Manitoshaw! I am here!'

"She at once recognized the voice and found it to be Nawakewee, who told a strange story. That morning a canoe had crossed the Wanagiska, carrying two men. They were Sioux. The old grandmother had seen them coming, and to deceive them she at once pulled down her temporary wigwam, and drove the ponies off toward home. Then she hid herself in the bushes nearby, for she knew that Manitoshaw must return there.

" 'Come, my granddaughter, we must hasten home by another way,' cried the old woman.

"But the maiden said, 'No, let us go first to my two moose that I killed this morning and take some meat with us.'

" 'No, no my child; the Sioux are cruel. They have killed many of our people. If we stay here they will find us. I fear, I fear them, Manitoshaw!'

"At last the brave maid convinced her grandmother, and

the more easily as she too was hungry for meat. They went to where the big game lay among the bushes, and began to dress the moose."

"I think, if I were they, I would hide all day. I would wait until the Sioux had gone; then I would go back to my moose," I interrupted for the third time.

"I will finish my story first; then you may tell us what you would do," said my uncle reprovingly.

"The two Sioux were father and son. They too had come to the lake for moose; but as the game usually retreated to the island, Chatansapa had landed his son Kangiska to hunt them on the shore while he returned in his canoe to intercept their flight. The young man sped along the sandy beach and soon discovered their tracks. He followed them up and found blood on the trail. This astonished him. Cautiously he followed on until he found them both lying dead. He examined them and found that in each moose there was a single Cree arrow. Wishing to surprise the hunter if possible, Kangiska lay hidden in the bushes.

"After a little while the two women returned to the spot. They passed him as close as the moose had passed the maiden in the morning. He saw at once that the maiden had arrows in her quiver like those that had slain the big moose. He lay still.

"Kangiska looked upon the beautiful Cree maiden and loved her. Finally he forgot himself and made a slight motion. Manitoshaw's quick eye caught the little stir among the bushes, but she immediately looked the other way and Kangiska believed that she had not seen anything. At last her eyes met his, and something told both that all was well. Then the maiden smiled, and the young man could not remain still any longer. He arose suddenly and the old woman nearly fainted from fright. But Manitoshaw said:

" 'Fear not, grandmother; we are two and he is only one.'

"While the two women continued to cut up the meat, Kangiska made a fire by rubbing cedar chips together, and they all ate of the moose meat. Then the old woman finished her work, while the young people sat down upon a log in the shade, and told each other all their minds.

"Kangiska declared by signs that he would go home with Manitoshaw to the Cree camp, for he loved her. They went home, and the young man hunted for the unfortunate Cree band during the rest of his life.

"His father waited a long time on the island and afterward searched the shore, but never saw him again. He supposed that those footprints he saw were made by Crees who had killed his son."

"Is that story true, uncle?" I asked eagerly.

"Yes, the facts are well known. There are some Sioux mixed bloods among the Crees to this day who are descendants of Kangiska."

THE POOR TURKEY GIRL

Long, long ago, our ancients had neither sheep nor horses nor cattle; yet they had domestic animals of various kinds—amongst them Turkeys.

In Matsaki, or Salt City, there dwelt at this time many very wealthy families, who possessed large flocks of these birds, which it was their custom to have their slaves or the poor people of the town herd in the plains round about Thunder Mountain, below which their town stood, and on the mesas beyond.

Now, in Matsaki at this time there stood, away out near the border of the town, a little tumbledown, single-room house, wherein there lived alone a very poor girl, so poor that her clothes were patched and tattered and dirty, and her person, on account of long neglect and ill-fare, shameful to look upon, though she herself was not ugly, but had a winning face and bright eyes; that is, if the face had been more oval and the eyes

(Excerpt from Frank H. Cushing, *Zuni Folk Tales*, G. P. Putnam's Sons, New York, 1901)

less oppressed with care. So poor was she that she herded Turkeys for a living; and little was given to her except the food she subsisted on from day to day, and perhaps now and then a piece of old, worn-out clothing.

Like the extremely poor everywhere and at all times, she was humble, and by her longing for kindness, which she never received, she was made kind even to the creatures that depended upon her, and lavished this kindness upon the Turkeys she drove to and from the plains every day. Thus, the Turkeys, appreciating this, were very obedient. They loved their mistress so much that at her call they would unhesitating come, or at her behest go wheresoever and whensoever she wished.

One day this poor girl, driving her Turkeys down into the plains, passed near Old Zuni—the Middle Ant Hill of the World, as our ancients have taught us to call our home—and as she went along, she heard the herald-priest proclaiming from the house-top that the Dance of the Sacred Bird (which is a very blessed and welcome festival to our people, especially to the youths and maidens who are permitted to join in the dance) would take place in four days.

Now, this poor girl had never been permitted to join in or even to watch the great festivities of our people or the people in the neighboring towns, and naturally she longed very much to see this dance. But she put aside her longing, because she reflected: "It is impossible that I should watch, much less join in the Dance of the Sacred Bird, ugly and ill-clad as I am." And thus musing to herself, and talking to her Turkeys, as was her custom, she drove them on, and at night returned them to their cages round the edges and in the plazas of the town.

Every day after that, until the day named for the dance, this poor girl, as she drove her Turkeys out in the morning, saw the people busy in cleaning and preparing their garments, cooking delicacies, and otherwise making ready for the festival to which they had been duly invited by the other villagers, and heard them talking and laughing merrily at the prospect of the coming holiday. So, as she went about with her Turkeys through the day, she would talk to them, though she never dreamed that they understood a word of what she was saying.

It seems that they did understand even more than she said to them, for on the fourth day, after the people of Matsaki had all departed toward Zuni and the girl was wandering around the plains alone with her Turkeys, one of the big Gobblers strutted up to her, and making a fan of his tail, and skirts, as it were, of his wings, blushed with pride and puffed with importance, stretched out his neck and said: "Maiden mother, we know what your thoughts are, and truly we pity you, and wish that, like the other people of Matsaki, you might enjoy this holiday in the town below. We have said to ourselves at night, after you have placed us safely and comfortably in our cages: 'Truly our maiden mother is as worthy to enjoy these things as any one in Matsaki, or even Zuni.'

"Now listen well, for I speak the speech of all the elders of my people: If you will drive us in early this afternoon, when the dance is most gay and the people are most happy, we will help you to make yourself so handsome and so prettily dressed that never a man, woman, or child amongst all those who are assembled at the dance will know you; but rather, especially the young men, will wonder whence you came, and long to lay hold of your hand in the circle that forms round the altar to dance. Maiden mother, would you like to go to see this dance, and even to join in it, and be merry with the best of your people?"

The poor girl was at first surprised. Then it seemed all so natural that the Turkeys should talk to her as she did to them, that she sat down on a little mound, and, leaning over, looked at them and said: "My beloved Turkeys, how glad I am that we may speak together! But why should you tell me of things that you full well know I so long to, but cannot by any possible means, do?"

"Trust in us," said the old Gobbler, "for I speak the speech of my people, and when we begin to call and call and gobble and gobble, and turn toward our home in Matsaki, do you follow us, and we will show you what we can do for you. Only let me tell you one thing: No one knows how much happiness and good fortune may come to you if you but enjoy temperately the pleasures we enable you to participate in. But if, in the excess of your enjoyment, you should forget us, who are your friends, yet so much depend upon you, then we will think: 'Behold, this our maiden mother, though so humble and poor, deserves, forsooth, her hard life, because, were she more prosperous, she would be unto others as others now are unto her.' "

"Never fear, O my Turkeys," cried the maiden—only half trusting that they could do so much for her, yet longing to try—"never fear. In everything you direct me to do I will be obedient as you always have been to me."

The sun had scarce begun to decline, when the Turkeys of their own accord turned homeward, and the maiden followed them, light of heart. They knew their places well, and immediately ran to them. When all had entered, even their bare-legged children, the old Gobbler called to the maiden, saying: "Enter our house." She therefore went in. "Now maiden, sit down," said he, "and give to me and my companions, one by one, your articles of clothing. We will see if we cannot renew them."

The maiden obediently drew off the ragged old mantle that covered her shoulders and cast it on the ground before the speaker. He seized it in his beak, and spread it out, and picked and picked at it, then he trod upon it, and lowering his wings, began to strut back and forth over it. Then taking it up in his beak, and continuing to strut, he puffed and puffed, and laid it down at the feet of the maiden, a beautiful white embroidered cotton mantle. Then another Gobbler came forth, and she gave him another article of dress, and then another and another, until each garment the maiden had worn was new and as beautiful as any possessed by her mistresses in Matsaki.

Before the maiden donned all these garments, the Turkeys circled about her, singing and singing, and clucking and clucking, and brushing her with their wings, until her person was as clean and her skin as smooth and bright as that of the fairest

maiden of the wealthiest home in Matsaki. Her hair was soft
and wavy, instead of being an ugly, sun-burnt shock; her
cheeks were full and dimpled, and her eyes dancing with
smiles—for she now saw how true had been the words of the
Turkeys.

Finally, one old Turkey came forward and said: "Only the
rich ornaments worn by those who have many possessions are
lacking to thee, O maiden mother. Wait a moment. We have
keen eyes, and have gathered many valuable things, as such
things, being small, though precious, are apt to be lost from
time to time by men and maidens."

Spreading his wings, he trod round and round upon the
ground, throwing his head back, and laying his wattled beard
on his neck; and, presently beginning to crouch, he produced
in his beak a beautiful necklace; another Turkey brought forth
earrings, and so on, until all the proper ornaments appeared,
befitting a well-clad maiden of the olden days, and were laid at
the feet of the poor Turkey girl.

With these beautiful things she decorated herself, and,
thanking the Turkeys over and over, she started to go, and they
called out: "O maiden mother, leave open the wicket, for who
knows whether you will remember your Turkeys or not when
your fortunes are changed, and if you will not grow ashamed
that you have been the maiden mother of Turkeys? But we love
you, and would bring you to good fortune. Therefore, remember our words of advice, and do not tarry too long."

"I will surely remember, O my Turkeys!" answered the
maiden.

Hastily she sped away down the river path toward Zuni.
When she arrived there, she went in at the western side of the
town and through one of the long covered ways that lead into
the dance court. When she came just inside of the court, behold, every one began to look at her, and many murmurs ran
through the crowd, murmurs of astonishment at her beauty
and the richness of her dress, and the people were all asking
one another, "Whence comes this beautiful maiden?"

Not long did she stand there neglected. The chiefs of the dance, all gorgeous in their holiday attire, hastily came to her, and, with apologies for the incompleteness of their arrangements, though these arrangements were as complete as they possibly could be, invited her to join the youths and maidens dancing round the musicians and the altar in the center of the plaza.

With a blush and a smile and a toss of her hair over her eyes, the maiden stepped into the circle, and the finest youths among the dancers vied with one another for her hand. Her heart became light and her feet merry, and the music sped her breath to rapid coming and going, and the warmth swept over her face, and she danced and danced until the sun sank low in the west.

But, alas! in the excess of her enjoyment, she thought not of her Turkeys, or, if she thought of them, she said to herself, "How is this, that I should go away from the most precious consideration to my flock of gobbling Turkeys? I will stay a while longer, and just before the sun sets I will run back to them, that these people may not see who I am, and that I may have the joy of hearing them talk day after day and wonder who the girl was who joined in their dance."

So the time sped on, and another dance was called, and another, and never a moment did the people let her rest; but they would have her in every dance as they moved around the musicians and the altar in the center of the plaza.

At last the sun set, and the dance was well-nigh over, when, suddenly breaking away, the girl ran out, and, being swift of foot, more so than most of the people of her village, she sped up the river path before any one could follow the course she had taken.

Meantime, as it grew late, the Turkeys began to wonder and wonder that their maiden mother did not return to them. At last a gray old Gobbler mournfully exclaimed, "It is as we might have expected. She has forgotten us; therefore is she not worthy of better things than those she has been accustomed to.

Let us go forth to the mountains and endure no more of this irksome captivity, inasmuch as we may no longer think our maiden mother as good and true as once we thought her."

So, calling and calling to one another in loud voices, they trooped out of their cage and ran up toward the Canyon of the Cottonwoods, and then round behind Thunder Mountain, through the Gateway of Zuni, and so on up the valley.

All breathless, the maiden arrived at the open wicket and looked in. Behold, not a Turkey was there! Trailing them, she ran and she ran up the valley to overtake them; but they were far ahead, and it was only after a long time that she came within the sound of their voices, and then, redoubling her speed, well-nigh overtook them, when she heard them singing a song.

Hearing this, the maiden called to her Turkeys; called and called in vain. They only quickened their steps, spreading their wings to help them along, singing their song over and over until they came to the base of Canyon Mesa, at the borders of the Zuni Mountains. Then singing once more their song in full chorus, they spread wide their wings, and fluttered away over the plains above.

The poor Turkey girl threw her hands up and looked down at her dress. With dust and sweat, behold! it was changed to what it had been, and she was the same poor Turkey girl that she was before. Weary, grieving, and despairing, she returned to Matsaki.

Thus it was in the days of the ancients. Therefore, where you see the rocks leading up to the top of Canyon Mesa, there are the tracks of Turkeys and other figures to be seen. The latter are the song that the Turkeys sang, graven in the rocks; and all over the plains along the borders of Zuni Mountains since that day turkeys have been more abundant than in any other place.

COYOTE AND THE
FAWN'S STARS

Once Coyote was out walking.
He was walking in the forest.
He met a deer. She had her baby with her.

Coyote said, "Hello, my cousin.
What pretty stars your baby has
on his back.
I wish my children had pretty stars."

Deer said, "Your babies can have stars.
I will tell you.
This is what I do.

When my babies are very little,
I build a big fire.
The sparks from the fire make the stars.
You can do that for your babies.
Then they will have pretty stars, too."

Coyote was happy.
Now he knew what to do.
He wanted his babies to have pretty stars.
He gathered wood.
He made a big fire.
He put all of his children in the fire.
The sparks flew.
"Now they will have pretty stars," said Coyote.

He danced around the fire.
Soon he said to Deer,
"Have they been in the fire long enough?"
"Yes," said Deer.
She ran away laughing.

Coyote took his children from the fire.
They were burned. They were dead.
Coyote was angry.
He chased Deer.
Coyote still chases Deer, but he
never catches her.

(Excerpt from Robert Young and William Morgan, *Coyote Tales*, Navajo Life Series, Bureau of Indian Affairs, Haskell Institute, Lawrence, Kansas, 1949)

COYOTE AND CROW

One day Coyote was out walking.
He saw Crow.
Crow was holding his hat under his foot.
"What is under your hat?" asked Coyote.
"I have a bluebird under my hat," said Crow.
"Will you hold it for me a little while," asked Crow.
"I will hold it," said Coyote.
"Don't look under it," said Crow.
"Don't let the bluebird get away."
"I will hold it," said Coyote.
"I will hold it until you get back."

Crow flew away.
He flew behind a rock.
He could see Coyote, but Coyote could not see him.

Coyote looked all around.
He did not see Crow.
He looked at the hat.
"A bluebird," he thought.
"A nice bluebird.
Crow is gone.

I'll eat the bluebird."
He looked around again.
He raised the hat carefully.
He grabbed—but it wasn't
a bluebird.
It was a cactus.

"Caw, caw, caw," said Crow from the tip of the rock.

Coyote was angry.
He sat down to pick the thorns out of his foot.
"Caw, caw, caw," said Crow again and flew away.

(Excerpt from Robert Young and William Morgan, *Coyote Tales*, Navajo Life Series, Bureau of Indian Affairs, Haskell Institute, Lawrence, Kansas, 1949)

BLACKFOOT LEGEND OF NAPI AND THE GREAT SPIRIT

There was once a Great Spirit who was good. He made a man and a woman. Then Napi came along. No one made Napi; he always existed. The Great Spirit said to him, "Napi, have you any power?" "Yes," said Napi, "I am very strong." "Well," said the Great Spirit, "suppose you make some mountains." So Napi set to work and made the Sweetgrass Hills. To do this he took a piece of Chief Mountain. He brought Chief Mountain up to its present location, shaped it up, and named it. The other mountains were called Blood Clots. "Well," said the Great Spirit, "you are strong."

"Now," said Napi, "there are four of us—the man and woman, you and I." The Great Spirit said, "All right."

(Excerpt from American Museum of Natural History, *Anthropological Papers*, vol. 2, New York, 1909)

The Great Spirit said, "I will make a big cross for you to carry." Napi said, "No, you make another man so that he can carry it." The Great Spirit made another man. Napi carried the cross a while but soon got tired and wanted to go. The Great Spirit told him that he could go, but he should go out among the people and the animals, and teach them how to live, and so forth.

Now the other man got tired of carrying the cross. He was a white man. The Great Spirit sent him off as a traveler. So he wandered on alone. The man and woman who had been created wandered off down towards Mexico, where they tried to build a mountain in order to get to the sky to be with their children; but the people got mixed up until they came to have many different languages.

NAPI AND THE ELK SKULL

One day Napi was going along, when he came to an elk skull on the ground. Inside of it were some mice dancing. Napi began to cry, because he wanted to go in and dance with the mice. The mice told him that he was too big to get in and dance, but that he could stick his head inside, and shake it which would be the same as dancing. "However," they said, "whatever you do, you must not go to sleep."

So, Napi stuck his head into the skull; but he forgot and went to sleep, and while he slept, the mice chewed all his hair off. When Napi awoke, he could not get the skull off his head, so he went into the river and swam along, with the antlers sticking up out of the water.

In this way he passed a camp of Indians. Then he made a noise like an elk. The people shot at him, went into the water and dragged him out; but when they had him on shore they saw that it was Napi. Then they took a stone and broke the skull, that he might get his head out again.

(Excerpt from American Museum of Natural History, *Anthropological Papers*, vol. 2, New York, 1909)

NAPI MAKES BUFFALO LAUGH

Napi looked from Red Deer River over to Little Bow River. He saw some buffalo. He tied up his hair in knots, and crawled along on hands and knees. The sight made the buffalo laugh. One of them laughed himself to death, and Napi butchered him.

(Excerpt from American Museum of Natural History, *Anthropological Papers*, vol. 2, New York, 1909)

ORIGIN OF NAMES
AMONG THE CHEROKEES

Among the interesting legends of the Cherokees is the one concerning the naming of children after animals and birds.

Long ago, when all Indians belonged to one great family, the children were not named until they were old enough to kill a certain number of the animals after which they wished to be named. The larger and fiercer the animal or bird, the more sought was its name. Thus the bear, wolf, eagle, and hawk were considered very good names, and those possessing these names were supposed to be endowed with great skill and prowess as hunters and warriors.

During this period there lived a young chief, Eg-wah Wi-yuh, whose greatest ambition was to be the father of a brave son—brave enough to earn the name of some fierce animal. At the birth of his first child he was greatly disappointed to find that he was born blind. So grieved was he over his afflicted son that for five days he neither ate nor drank anything; neither did he allow anyone to enter his tipi. On the fifth night he fell into unconsciousness, and while in this condition a large bird en-

(A legend told by Sylvester Long for *The Red Man*, student newspaper of the Carlisle Indian School, Carlisle, Pennsylvania, ca. 1925)

tered his tipi and carried him away. He awoke to find himself sailing through the air on the back of a large bird. He had not been awake long before he discovered that they were traveling toward the moon, which already appeared many times larger than he had before seen it. On reaching the moon he was surprised to discover that instead of being the planet which he thought it to be, it was, in reality, a large opening in a thick black crust. After passing through the moon, he saw on the other side, men walking around with large holes in their heads instead of eyes. On regaining his faculties he asked the bird what all this meant and where he was being carried.

He was told that he had died and his spirit was being carried to Guh-luh-lau-eeh—Happy Hunting Grounds—to be judged and sent back to the place they had just passed. The bird, on being further questioned, explained that this place was built by the Great Spirit and intended for the spirits of animals and birds, but owing to the cruel custom of killing animals for their names, the Great Spirit had sent a curse upon the Indians. He had given the animals the real Happy Hunting Grounds and driven the spirits of the Indians to the place which they had just passed, to have their eyes eaten out by the birds, and tormented by the animals they had wantonly killed on earth for the sake of assuming their titles.

He was informed that they were on the way to Guh-luh-lau-eeh, the real Happy Hunting Grounds, where the chief of the animals and birds dwelt, which was reached by passing through the sun. The moon, he said, was for the wicked spirits of the Indians to pass through during the night, and the sun for the spirits of the animals to pass through during the day. The Great Spirit covered the earth with the black sheet long enough for the evil spirits to pass into their torment, and the white one long enough for the spirits of the animals and birds to pass into Guh-luh-lau-eeh, thereby producing day and night.

On passing through the sun he was amazed at the beauty of the place. He was carried to the large wigwam of the Great

Chief of the animal and bird kingdom. On discovering that his subject was not dead, but had merely fallen into a stupor, from which he had already recovered, he was greatly annoyed and ordered the bird to carry Eg-wah Wi-yuh to the fiercest animals of the kingdom to be devoured and his spirit sent to the land of evil spirits to be tormented by the animals and birds.

Wi-yuh asked if there was anything he could do to save himself. The Great Chief told him yes, there was one thing he could do to save himself, and that was to go back to the earth and abolish the custom of slaying innocent animals and birds for their names. He told Wi-yuh that if he accomplished this one task he would make him ruler of the animal and bird kingdom, and would give back to the spirits of the Indians Guh-luh-lau-eeh, and allow them to hunt as much as they wanted among all the animals and birds in that kingdom. He promised that if the young chief would name his blind child after the first animal or bird he would see on looking from his tipi the next morning after returning to his home, instead of adhering to the old custom and thereby set an example for the other Indians to follow, he would cause the child to gain its eyesight.

On returning to the earth Wi-yuh told his people all that had happened and they did not believe him, but the next morning when he named his child for the first animal he saw when he looked from his tepee, his son instantly gained his eyesight. Everyone now believed him, and from that day to within recent years, the Indians have named their children after the first object they saw on looking from their tepees when a child was born.

The following day Wi-yuh disappeared to Guh-luh-lau-eeh.

WHY THE TURKEY IS BALD

The Indians of our country have many legends connected with certain peculiar habits or customs prevalent among them. If one should chance to visit the home of an old Indian he would perhaps notice a turkey wing hanging near the fire. This the Indian uses to fan his fire into a flame and make it burn brightly, or perhaps in the sultry days of summer, to fan himself. If asked why he uses the turkey wing instead of the wing of any other bird, he would no doubt relate the following story:

Many years ago the fire of the world was nearly extinguished; this happened just at the beginning of the winter season. The birds of the air were filled with anxiety, for their intuition told them they would need heat to keep them warm through the winter.

A bird council was held and it was decided that birds which could fly the highest should soar into the air and see if they could find a spark of fire anywhere. The efforts of the eagle, lark and raven were in vain. The honor was left to the little brown sparrow, who spied a spark of fire in the hollow of an old stump, in the heart of a deep forest.

The birds flocked around the stump and tried to decide who should pick the spark out. But all their efforts were in vain; to their dismay they saw the spark growing smaller and fainter. The turkey then volunteered to try and keep the tiny coal alive by fanning it with his wings. Day after day the turkey kept fanning; the heat became greater each day, until the feathers were singed off the turkey's head. If one notices carefully he will see lumps on the head of a turkey that appear as blisters. It is believed that the turkey was so badly burned that all turkeys since have had bald heads and wear the blisters as a memento of the bravery of the turkey. The faithful turkey lost his beautiful feathers but he gave back fire to the world; so in

---

(By Nan Saunooke, Cherokee, excerpted from *The Red Man*, Carlisle Indian School student newspaper, ca. 1925)